# High-Tech WARFARE

ROBERT JACKSON

# High-Tech WARFARE
## The Weaponry Explained

HEADLINE

Text copyright © Robert Jackson1991
Drawings copyright © Eddison Sadd Editions 1991
This edition copyright © Eddison Sadd Editions 1991

First published in 1991
by HEADLINE BOOK PUBLISHING PLC

The right of Robert Jackson to be identified as the author of
the work has been asserted by him in accordance with the
Copyright, Designs and Patents Act 1988

10 9 8 7 6 5 4 3 2 1

British Library Cataloguing in Publication Data
Jackson, Robert, *1941-*
 High-tech warfare.
 I. Title
 355.8

ISBN 0 7472 0509 4

AN EDDISON • SADD EDITION
Edited, designed and produced by
Eddison Sadd Editions Limited
St Chad's Court
146B Kings Cross Road
London WC1X 9DH

Phototypeset in Garamond and Franklin
Gothic by Wyvern Typesetting Ltd, Bristol

Origination by Columbia Offset, Singapore

Printed and bound by Eurograph spa, Italy

HEADLINE BOOK PUBLISHING PLC
Headline House
79 Great Titchfield Street
London WlP 7FN

Title page: *The nerve centre of a modern aircraft carrier where technology plays a crucial role in the air,
on the sea, as well as under it.*
Opposite: *A Los Angeles-class nuclear submarine surfaces after a tour of the Earth's oceans, quietly
listening and waiting...*
Contents page: *Members of the RAF Regiment stand guard over a Tornado GR1 in Operation Desert
Storm. For many new weapons, the Gulf War was a proving ground as well as a test bench.*

# CONTENTS

# INTRODUCTION

**D**URING the 1970s and '90s, prior to the collapse of the Warsaw Pact, the military planners of the North Atlantic Treaty Organization were faced with massive Soviet superiority in manpower and materials. In response, they focused on providing NATO forces with the most modern high-technology weapons as a means of redressing the balance of power.

That policy was a valid one, for in the Gulf War the use of high-tech weapons - many of them never before proven in action - broke Iraq's military spine and saved the lives of countless Allied soldiers.

The Gulf War was won by smart weapons operated by smart people. But weapons alone do not achieve victories. Even though the NATO military command was absent from the Gulf, its influence was clearly felt. The military coalition that had trained together for four decades in preparation for a massive war in Europe put its expertise to work in the fight against Iraq, with ground, air and naval forces operating under unified command, in much the same way as they would have done in battle on NATO's central front.

The success of high-technology weaponry in Operation Desert Storm was greeted almost euphorically by those who had advocated its development over the years. But it should not be forgotten that Iraq, for all its apparent military might, is a Third World nation, and that many assessments of its military capability were based on its long war with another Third World country, Iran. When Iraq found itself confronted with the best-trained, best-equipped armed forces in the world, it was utterly outclassed.

In this context, there are inherent dangers in over-estimating the effectiveness of high-technology weapons. The widespread deployment of the latest weaponry may permit sweeping reductions in armoured and infantry forces - as is happening today in European NATO - but it can never replace them. What it can do is help mould a new-style military force, one capable of reacting very rapidly to any threat, anywhere in the world. The need for such an integrated, powerfully-armed force is one of the key lessons to emerge from the Gulf War.

The purpose of this book is not only to examine the whole spectrum of high-tech weaponry - some already tested in combat, some still under intensive development - but also to look at how it is employed operationally, and what effect it is likely to have on future wars and those compelled to fight them. If there is a conclusion to be drawn, it is that the deterrent effect of high-tech weapons is a major stabilizing factor in a highly unstable world.

*Opposite: A mother and her son investigate some of the high-tech weaponry used during the Gulf War, at an air base open day.*

# PART ONE

# AIR WAR 2000

*A Canadian CF-18 Hornet of the Canadian Armed Forces soars skywards.*

# CHAPTER ONE

# THE INTERCEPTORS

**T**HE *concept of what is nowadays called the interceptor fighter originated early in the 1914-18 war, when commanders on both sides began to recognize the urgent need to destroy enemy reconnaissance aircraft before the latter could escape with vital information on troop movements, artillery positions, and trench systems. By early 1915 the Allies and the Germans had both instituted standing patrols in the vicinity of the front line, especially in sectors opposite airfields that were to be used by reconnaissance machines.*

As bombing attacks on the British mainland by German Zeppelins increased, a system of home defence squadrons was created by the Royal Flying Corps, but because of the demands of the Western Front these were given second-rate equipment, elderly aircraft such as the Be 2c, which were hard-pressed to reach the Zeppelins'

The most potent Allied piston-engined interceptor of the Second World War was Britain's Hawker Tempest which could catch Me 262 jet fighters.

*operating altitudes. It was not until early 1918 that the RFC's home defence squadrons were registering regular successes against both airships and heavier-than-air bombers, and by that time the German bombing offensive was tailing off.*

*The lessons learned in the operation of that early air defence system, especially with regard to its inadequacies, were not forgotten in the 1930s when Great Britain once again faced a formidable military threat from Germany. By the outbreak of the 1939-45 war, the British air defence system was without question the finest in the world, with the operational airfields of RAF Fighter Command grouped into key sectors, and its Spitfire and Hurricane squadrons tactically controlled by radar, the secret weapon that was to play such a vital role in winning the Battle of Britain.*

*Radar gave the RAF's fighter squadrons the advantage they needed to intercept enemy bomber formations out at sea as they flew towards their targets. It also, eventually, led to the formation of an effective RAF night interceptor force, although airborne radar development was beset by early difficulties.*

*By the end of the Second World War, the interceptor concept had entered a new dimension with the advent of jet fighters like Germany's Messerschmitt 262 and Britain's Gloster Meteor. The Me 262 was the more advanced of the two, with a higher performance and a heavy armament of four 30 mm cannon and 24 air-to-air rockets.*

*The post-war years saw the emergence of a fearsome new challenge for the interceptor: the nuclear-armed jet bomber. More than ever, it became vital for interceptions to be carried out far from friendly territory, and this gave rise to a new generation of long-range interceptors - aircraft such as the USAF's F-101, F-102, and F-106 , and the Soviet Tupolev Tu-28. The RAF,*

whose principal interceptors of the early 1960s - the Lightning and Javelin - had shorter ranges, opted for flight refuelling as a means of extending endurance.

By the mid-1960s, advances in radar, defensive surface-to-air missiles and interception techniques had forced the nuclear-armed bomber to fly low, hiding its radar signature behind the terrain, if it was to have a chance of survival. Most strategic bombers were now armed with some form of stand-off weaponry - the RAF had the combination of Vulcan bomber and Blue Steel missiles, for example - so that it now became imperative for interceptors to destroy the bombers before they reached missile firing range. They also had to be able to intercept large numbers of aircraft approaching their targets at high speed and at very low level.

These requirements led to the development of the modern generation of interceptors equipped with airborne radar capable of tracking a number of

The RAF made extensive use of in-flight refuelling to extend the range of its interceptors. Here a Victor K2 refuels a pair of Lightnings.

targets simultaneously, and armed with weapons able to engage the enemy force far beyond visual range.

America produced the McDonnell Douglas F-15 Eagle for the USAF and the Grumman F-14 Tomcat for the US Navy. Both aircraft were equipped with a formidable missile armament. France continued the development of its well-proven Mirage line, creating the Mirage 2000 and 4000. Britain's answer was the Panavia Tornado F3. It has been developed to meet an RAF air defence requirement for a combat air patrol capability far out over the northern waters, but was called to action stations in the very different and more demanding environment of the Gulf.

# BLOWING UP A STORM The Tornado strikes

**F**OLLOWING the Iraqi invasion of Kuwait in August 1990, one of the first Allied moves during the Desert Shield phase of operations - the progressive buildup of forces in the Gulf area - involved the deployment of RAF Tornado F3 aircraft to Saudi Arabia.

The Tornados' task - although less exciting than that of their USAF F-15 counterparts, which was to fly escort to strike aircraft and seek out and destroy the Iraqi Air Force - was nevertheless demanding and vital to the success of Allied operations. It was to defend the Saudi Arabian bases against Iraqi air attack, and to fly combat air patrols along the lengthy Saudi-Iraq frontier, ready to intercept raids by enemy aircraft. In the event, no such incursions took place.

Only on one occasion were the Tornados ordered to intercept a hostile aircraft, but it turned away and fled northwards before they came within missile firing range.

### GOVERNMENTAL BRIEFING

The Panavia Tornado ADV (Air Defence Variant) was developed to replace the British Aerospace Lightning and, in part, the MacDonnell Douglas F-4 Phantom in the air defence of the United Kingdom. Its systems are common to those of the Tornado GRI strike aircraft, with the addition of air defence radar equipment. The requirement dates back to 1971, when it was seen as the most cost-effective means of countering a new breed of Soviet strike aircraft like the Sukhoi Su-24 Fencer.

At that time, as part of a NATO/Warsaw Pact war scenario, it was envisaged that aircraft such as the Su-24, perhaps operating from captured airfields in northern Norway, would have posed a serious threat to bases in the United Kingdom and to naval operations in the North Norwegian Sea, the control of which would have been crucial to the outcome of any conflict. The Tornado ADV's area of operations was to cover a great sweep of sky extending from the English Channel to the Iceland-Faeroes-UK Gap.

The aircraft that eventually emerged was a long-range interceptor, with lengthy combat air patrol (CAP) endurance, capable of engaging multiple targets in rapid succession, in all weathers and in complex, electronic countermeasures (ECM) conditions. It was designed to operate with the

*A Tornado F3 fitted with long-range fuel tanks peels away from the aircraft camera.*

United Kingdom Air Defence System, airborne early warning aircraft, tankers and air defence ships, all linked on a secure ECM-resistant data and voice command and control network.

The Tornado ADV's intercept radar is the GEC Marconi Avionics AI24 Foxhunter. Despite early development problems, the Foxhunter now meets all its requirements. It can detect targets at an initial range of about 100 nautical miles; these are stored in the aircraft's central digital computer which analyzes the principal threats while the radar continues to scan and display new targets to the two-man crew, keeping up a 'running commentary' on ranges, velocities and tracks. With the computer fully updated, the crew plan their approach to engage the maximum number of targets.

As its main armament, the Tornado ADV carries four British Aerospace Dynamics Sky Flash air-to-air missiles. Developed from the US AIM-7E

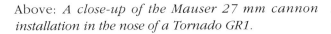

Above: *A close-up of the Mauser 27 mm cannon installation in the nose of a Tornado GR1.*

Above and top left: *The F3 equips seven RAF squadrons and carries a formidable weapons package.*

Sparrow, Sky Flash has a range of about 30 nautical miles and is a semi-active radar homing weapon. The missile's radar seeker is integrated with the aircraft's radar system and can separate a close formation of aircraft into individuals, selecting one for attack.

Secondary armament, for closer-range work, is the AIM-9L Sidewinder, of which four are carried on underwing stations, and for really close-range combat the aircraft carries a built-in 27 mm Mauser cannon. Other missile options which will be available for the Tornado in the future are the AIM-120 AMRAAM or the AIM-132 ASRAAM, the latter envisaged as a replacement for the Sidewinder.

## THE OTHER VARIANT

The first Tornado IDVs entered service with No 229 Operational Conversion Unit at RAF Coningsby,

Lincolnshire, in November 1984. The first 18 aircraft were designated Tornado F2s and subsequent aircraft, with more powerful Turbo-Union RBl99 Mk 104 turbofan engines, were designated F3. The aircraft today equips seven squadrons of RAF Strike Command in the air defence role.

The Tornado F3 can remain airborne, without refuelling, for over four hours. It is capable of Mach 2.2 at high level, and more than 800 knots at low level.

The role of the Tornado F3 is changing. The advent of the very highly agile Soviet long-range combat aircraft like the Sukhoi Su-27 Flanker means that it must be capable of dogfighting, a role which it was never designed to assume. In this respect, it is a very different aircraft from the American interceptor with which it operated closely in the Gulf War - the McDonnell Douglas F-15C Eagle.

# F-15 AND MIG 29 A duel of eagles

OF the 39 Iraqi aircraft destroyed in air combat during the Gulf War, no fewer than 30 were shot down by one interceptor type, the McDonnell Douglas F-15C Eagle, deployed to Saudi Arabia with the United States Air Force's 33rd and 36th Tactical Fighter Wings in the vanguard of Operation Desert Shield. The majority of the air-to-air 'kills' were made with the F-15C's primary armament, the Raytheon/General Dynamics AIM-7 Sparrow.

The F-15 Eagle was developed in the mid-1960s under conditions of great urgency to counter the threat posed by the Soviet Air Force's MiG-25 Foxbat interceptor. The aircraft's appearance came as a shock to NATO and was itself developed to meet a potential threat from a new generation of US strategic bombers, like the North American XB-70 Valkyrie. The first F-15A Eagle was delivered to the USAF in November 1974, and deliveries of operational aircraft were made in the following year to the 57th and 58th Tactical Fighter Training Wings.

## A SIMPLE BRIEF - TO PRODUCE THE BEST

The F-15 Eagle was designed to out-perform, out-fly and out-fight any enemy aircraft in the foreseeable future. Its light wing loading, combined with the power of its two 25,000 lbs thrust, Pratt & Whitney advanced technology turbofans, gives it an extraordinary turning ability and the combat thrust-to-weight ratio necessary to retain the initiative in a fight. This high thrust-to-weight ratio permits a 'scramble' time of only six seconds, using 600 ft of runway, and a maximum speed of more than Mach 2.5. This gives the pilot the margin he needs if he has to break off a combat and run for safety.

The F-15 carries four AIM-7F Sparrow air-to-air missiles which are radar-guided and have a range of up to 35 miles. These are backed up by four AIM-9L Sidewinders for shorter-range interceptions and a General Electric 20 mm M61 rotary-barrel cannon for close-in combat. The Eagle's APG-63 pulse-Doppler air-to-air radar provides a good look-down capability and can be used in a variety of ways. It can pick up Phantom-sized targets at around 100 miles range and, in the radar's raid assessment mode, can resolve close formations into individual targets, as can the Tornado F 3's Foxhunter radar.

F-15s were supplied to the Israeli Air Force and scored some spectacular successes over Lebanon in 1982, when they engaged a variety of Syrian aircraft, including high-flying MiG-25R recon-naissance aircraft. The Eagle's radar has a mode called velocity search; when this is selected the radar shows only

*The McDonnell Douglas F-15 Eagle, one of the world's most powerful interceptors. The Eagle was responsible for most of the air-to-air kills of the Gulf War.*

## EYEBALL AND SHOOTER

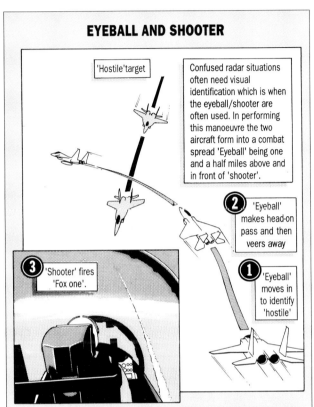

'Hostile' target

Confused radar situations often need visual identification which is when the eyeball/shooter are often used. In performing this manoeuvre the two aircraft form into a combat spread 'Eyeball' being one and a half miles above and in front of 'shooter'.

② 'Eyeball' makes head-on pass and then veers away

③ 'Shooter' fires 'Fox one'.

① 'Eyeball' moves in to identify 'hostile'

The Eyeball/Shooter method of combat is aimed at killing the enemy in the shortest possible time without becoming committed to a turning fight. The lead fighter makes a fast head-on pass to identify the enemy aircraft, and his wingman, who is some distance astern of the leader, fires a Sparrow AAM 'Fox One' from a direct head-on position. If the situation does break down into a turning fight, the Eagle pilots have the option of using their Sidewinder AAMs for a close-in 'Fox Two' shot, and finally their M61 cannon should all else fail.

target velocities at long range, so if the pilot sees a return that is flying at Mach 3 and 70,000 feet, and he hears no IFF (Identification Friend/Foe) signal being emitted from his IFF warning equipment, he can be fairly certain that he is dealing with a MiG-25R, and take appropriate steps to engage it.

### A FORMIDABLE RUSSIAN ADVERSARY

Russia's answer to the F-15 is the MiG-29 Fulcrum. Development of this agile combat aircraft began in 1969, and the type was first deployed with the Soviet Air Force early in 1985. The MiG-29's design emphasis is on manoeuvrability; when first displayed at air shows in the west, it startled observers by

carrying out a tail-slide manoeuvre never before performed by a high-performance combat aircraft. It later transpired that this was a specially developed combat manoeuvre, designed to break a Doppler radar lock.

The MiG-29 has a true look-down/shoot-down capability, with interlinked 62-mile range N0-93 pulse-Doppler radar, infra-red search and track sensor and helmet-mounted sights. Up to six AA-10 Alamo medium-range or eight AA-8 Aphid/AA-11 Archer short-range missiles can be carried. A single six-barrelled 30 mm cannon is also carried.

MiG-29s have been widely exported to the Soviet Union's principal customers, and in Iraqi Air Force service saw combat in the Gulf War - although in Iraqi hands they were no match for the USAF's F-15s. This formidable aircraft is also now in service with the German *Luftwaffe*, as a direct result of its unification in 1990.

*A Mig-29 Fulcrum pictured on take-off. The Fulcrum is an excellent Air Superiority fighter. Its aerodynamic qualities came as a shock to Western observers*

# THE EURO FIGHTER Into the 21st century

**T**HE highest priority in any country's armament programme in the years to come must remain its ability to defend the homeland with a high-performance fighter. That aircraft is EFA, the European Fighter Aircraft, which will begin equipping the air forces of Britain, Germany, Italy and Spain in the late 1990s.

### DEMONSTRATOR BLUEPRINT

EFA is the product of a four-nation consortium comprising British Aerospace, Aeritalia of Italy, CASA of Spain, and Germany's MBB and Dornier, working under the collective title of Eurofighter. To prove the necessary technology, British Aerospace built an agile demonstrator aircraft - not a prototype - called the Experimental Aircraft Programme, or EAP.

The EAP demonstrator flew for the first time on 8 August 1986, only three years after the programme was conceived. Powered by two Rolls-Royce RB 199 Mk 104D engines, it is the most advanced aircraft ever produced in Britain. The EAP's basic design owes much to a project known as the Agile Combat Aircraft, which was proposed in 1982 by Panavia, the consortium responsible for Tornado.

A single-seat delta-canard design, its design emphasis is on air combat performance, which in practice means a combination of high turn rates and high specific excess power, the measure of a fighter's ability to regain speed or altitude quickly after a combat manoeuvre. The result is a superb aircraft which, in effect, is the blueprint for EFA, the fighter that will project NATO's leading European air forces into the 21st century and provide them with the means to counter any foreseeable air threat that will be thrown against them.

### THE EUROFIGHTER ROLE

EFA's task will be to fight effectively throughout the combat spectrum, from engagements beyond visual range down to close-in combat. The technologies necessary to enable it to do this are so advanced, in some cases quite unique, that the role of the EAP demonstrator is vital to the EFA project as a whole.

In the air defence role, as soon as a hostile aircraft is detected beyond visual range, the EFA must accelerate from its combat air patrol (CAP) as quickly as possible to give its medium-range, fire-and-forget missiles maximum launch energy. It must

## A PLANE FROM ALL NATIONS

The first prototypes of the European Fighter Aircraft are taking shape in four different countries. The wings, made mainly of carbon fibre composite materials, are being constructed from parts made in Spain, Italy and the United Kingdom, and each major component for the first prototype is being shipped to Germany for final assembly at the MBB factory. British Aerospace is building the front fuselages, plus half of the right half of the wings; Germany's MBB is responsible for the centre fuselages, plus half of the vertical tail surfaces; Italy's AIT is constructing the left wings, plus half of the aft fuselage. The other half is being built by CASA of Spain, and they are also responsible for the right wings.

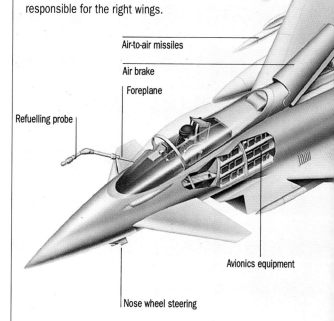

Air-to-air missiles

Air brake

Foreplane

Refuelling probe

Avionics equipment

Nose wheel steering

then manoeuvre hard, without losing energy itself, to force incoming enemy missiles to make violent course corrections towards the end of their flight, reducing their chances of scoring hits. This phase of the engagement therefore requires high acceleration and good supersonic manoeuvrability.

The next phase - close-in combat - requires maximum usable lift and a high thrust-to-weight ratio, so that energy lost in turns can quickly be regained. In this phase EFA will use all-aspect short-range weaponry, the engagement starting with fast head-on attacks and then breaking down into a turning fight, with pilots manoeuvring hard to

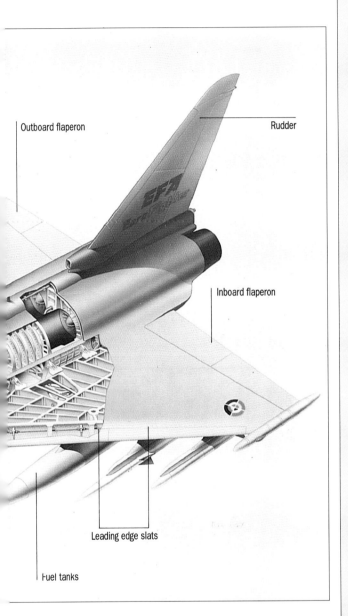

Outboard flaperon

Rudder

Inboard flaperon

Leading edge slats

Fuel tanks

## FINGERTIP TECHNOLOGY

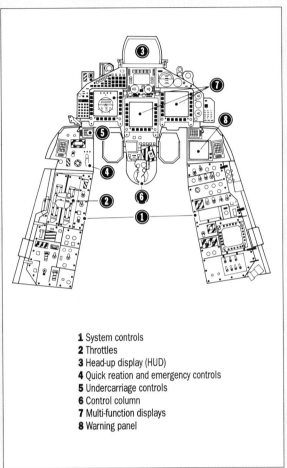

**1** System controls
**2** Throttles
**3** Head-up display (HUD)
**4** Quick reation and emergency controls
**5** Undercarriage controls
**6** Control column
**7** Multi-function displays
**8** Warning panel

EFA's cockpit features colour, head-down multi-function displays and a wide-angle holographic head-up display. Direct Voice Input (DVI) controls items such as radio channel changes and map displays, but not safety-critical systems such as weapon firing. The aircraft is fitted with an advanced pulse-Doppler radar, the ECR 90, developed by Euroradar, a consortium led by GEC Ferranti Defence Systems Ltd.

EFA is very much a pilot's aeroplane, with emphasis on the best possible all-round visibility and comfort during 'high-g' manoeuvres. One feature is the pilot's helmet-mounted sight, which avoids the need to pull tight turns to achieve missile lock-on. Pilots will also have a new fast-reacting g-suit to reduce the risk of g-induced loss of consciousness. These innovations mean that there will be no need to rake the EFA's ejection seat at more than the conventional 18-degree angle, which is good for the pilot's visibility. It also means that a centrally positioned control column can be retained (aircraft with highly raked seats, like the F-16, need a side-stick).

acquire good firing positions quickly. EFA's missiles will comprise the AIM-120 as the primary weapon, with the AIM-132 ASRAAM chosen as the secondary one. The aircraft will also have a built-in gun armament, probably the 27 mm Mauser.

Eight EFA prototypes are scheduled to be built, the first flying in 1991 and the others within a two-year span. The aircraft will be powered by two 20,000 lb thrust engines manufactured by Eurojet Turbo GmbH, a four-nation company. The requirement is for 765 EFAs, with 250 going to the RAF and *Luftwaffe* and 165 and 100 to the Italian and Spanish Air Forces respectively.

# CHAPTER TWO

# THE INTERDICTORS

THE *basic idea of interdiction - the severing of an enemy's lines of communication and supply, so preventing reinforcement of the battle area - is almost as old as air warfare itself. It was used on a large scale for the first time in the spring of 1918, when the Royal Flying Corps - which became the Royal Air Force on 1 April that year - launched a massive effort by both day and night, to slow down the German offensives on the Somme and Lys by attacking roads, railways and marshalling yards, bridges and other communications bottlenecks.*

*Specialized night interdiction was developed by the RAF in 1943, using de Havilland Mosquitoes of No 2 Group, and in the weeks preceding the Allied invasion of Normandy in 1944, the role was assumed by virtually the whole of the Allied strategic air forces, which mounted a massive and successful campaign against the enemy's transportation system.*

*During the Korean War, the principal*

A Martin B-57B of the USAF flying high over the continental United States, resplendent in an all-black night camouflage.

*interdictor aircraft was the Douglas B-26C Invader, which was later replaced in this role by the Martin B-57, a licence-built version of Britain's English Electric Canberra. The RAF also used two Canberra variants as interdictors and intruders, the B(I)6 and B(I)8; both carried an underwing bomb armament and a ventral 20 mm gun pack.*

*The USAF's Martin B-57Bs saw widespread service in Vietnam, beginning interdiction sorties against enemy supplies on the Ho Chi Minh Trail in April 1965. These missions were carried out in conjunction with C-130 or C-123 flare ships and EF-10B Skynight electronic warfare aircraft.*

*The highly specialized B-57G devolved from these operations. This aircraft, barely re-cognizable as a Canberra variant, carried a low light level TV system, forward-looking infra-red equipment and a laser guidance system, all of which were operated by a systems specialist in the aircraft's rear seat. The relevant information was fed by the systems operator into a computer and was displayed in the pilot's cockpit so that he could select the appropriate weapons combination.*

*The modified aircraft could carry the same ordnance as the B-57B, except that the laser guidance system now made it possible to fit four 500 lb 'smart' bombs bolted onto its underwing pylons.*

*Other aircraft used for interdiction work in Vietnam were the General Dynamics F-111 and the Grumman A-6 Intruder, both of which remain in today's USAF and US Navy's inventories. They are at the forefront of the role alongside the interdictor/strike Tornados of the RAF, the* Luftwaffe *and the Italian Air Force.*

*More recently, the role has also been assumed by the Lockheed F-117A 'Stealth' aircraft and the McDonnell Douglas F-15E Strike Eagle, both of which were used operationally in the Gulf War.*

*The F-117A is a single-seat, subsonic low-level strike, defence suppression and tactical reconnaissance aircraft, powered by two General Electric F404 turbofans with shielded exhausts, designed to dissipate heat emissions and so minimize the aircraft's infra-red signature. The use of faceting - angled flat surfaces - scatters incoming radar energy, while radar-absorbent materials and transparencies treated with conductive coating further reduce the F-117A's radar profile.*

*The use of modern technology, some of which can be applied retrospectively to existing airframes, like the Tornado's, to render a strike aircraft virtually invisible to enemy radar defences, is obviously the best solution to the problems faced by modern interdictors, because it enables them to operate at medium levels in the target area with minimum risk.*

*In times past, strike aircraft were forced to operate at extremely low levels in order to penetrate enemy defences. It was a very hazardous operation before the advent of automatic terrain-following radar. This system is linked to the aircraft's control system in much the same way as an automatic pilot flies it over and around obstacles, relieving the pilot of much of his workload. In modern interdictors like the F-111, the pilot can literally fly 'hands off' until the final phase of the low-level attack, when he must assume control manually in order to evade SAM and AAA defences.*

*Interdictor aircraft have to contend with an enormous variety of defensive systems arrayed against them before they reach their target areas. In breaking through this barrier they are assisted by a concept which, like so many others, was born in the Vietnam War - the anti-radar 'Wild Weasel' aircraft.*

This photograph clearly shows the sweep range of the General Dynamics F-111's wings. The lead aircraft has its wings fully swept for high-speed flight.

# THE 'WILD WEASELS' Breaching the electronic barrier

FROM mid-1965 onwards, USAF and USN strike aircraft operating over North Vietnam faced one of the most formidable air defence systems ever devised: a massive array of AAA guns, automatic weapons, SAMs and a modern interceptor force.

An electronic war developed between US tactical aircraft and the enemy's defensive complex, with United States EB-66 electronic warfare aircraft combining with F-100s or F-105s to detect emissions from an enemy 'Fan Song' radar - indicating that the launch of an SA-2 Guideline surface-to-air missile was imminent - and then destroy the installation with bombs or missiles. Aircraft tasked with these operations were given the code name 'Wild Weasels'.

As a result of the lessons learned in Vietnam, the provision of airborne equipment to fulfil the defence suppression role, and the modification of aircraft to carry it, assumed top priority in USAF Tactical Air Command planning in 1965. What TAC needed was a self-contained weapon system - an aircraft capable of carrying both the necessary electronics and the weaponry to hit enemy SAM radars effectively. The McDonnell Douglas F-4 Phantom was the best choice available. Wild Weasel trials had already been carried out with two F-4Ds in 1968, but later studies showed that the F-4E variant was easier to modify. USAF funding was consequently obtained to convert 116 of the F-4Es to F-4G standard under the Advanced Wild Weasel programme.

## UPDATING THE PHANTOM

Modifications included the addition of a torpedo-shaped fairing on top of the fin to house an APR-47 radar antenna, which is also carried on the side of the fin and along the upper surface of the fuselage. The F-4E's M61A1 cannon installation was removed to permit the installation of the computer systems associated with the F-4G's sensory radar. With this equipment, the Wild Weasel crew can detect, identify and locate hostile radar emissions and select the appropriate weapons system for use against them.

F-4G Wild Weasels can operate independently as 'hunter-killers', but more usually they operate as an integral component of a strike force. F-4Gs of the 35th Tactical Fighter Wing, normally based at George AFB in California, operated in support of Allied strike aircraft during Operation Desert Storm, using AGM-88 HARM high-speed anti-radiation missiles.

F-4Gs also equip the 81st Tactical Fighter Squadron, which is part of the 52nd Tactical Fighter Wing at Ramstein AB, Germany. F-16 Fighting

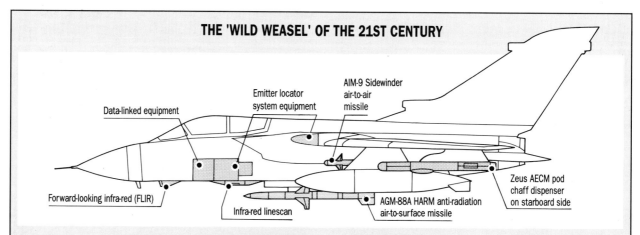

## THE 'WILD WEASEL' OF THE 21ST CENTURY

Data-linked equipment

Emitter locator system equipment

AIM-9 Sidewinder air-to-air missile

Forward-looking infra-red (FLIR)

Infra-red linescan

AGM-88A HARM anti-radiation air-to-surface missile

Zeus AECM pod chaff dispenser on starboard side

The Tornado ECR A 'Wild Weasel' version of the Panavia Tornado has been developed for service with the German *Luftwaffe*. Designed for both defence suppression and reconnaissance roles, the Tornado ECR is equipped with a Texas Instruments emitter location system (ELS) and infra-red sensors. For offensive operations the aircraft carries the AGM-88 HARM, while the reconnaissance function gathers information from all available sensors for instantaneous transmission to other aircraft or ground stations.

The Tornado ECR is being offered to the USAF as an F-4G replacement in the Wild Weasel role, but this seems unlikely due to the lack of available funding from Congress.

Falcons equipping the 52nd's other squadrons also have an interim HARM capability.

Outside the USA, only France, Israel and the Soviet Union operate dedicated 'Wild Weasel' aircraft.

The RAF's Tornado GR1s carry their own anti-radar missiles in the form of the BAe ALARM. Each Tornado can carry up to eight ALARMs, or air-launched-anti-radiation missiles, if the aircraft is used

*A HARM-equipped F-16 Fighting Falcon sits on the ramp at Ramstein AB where the United States Air Force in Europe has its headquarters.*

in the defence suppression role. ALARM was rushed into service during the Gulf War and was successfully used in the first wave of attacks on Iraq.

## FORCING A PATH

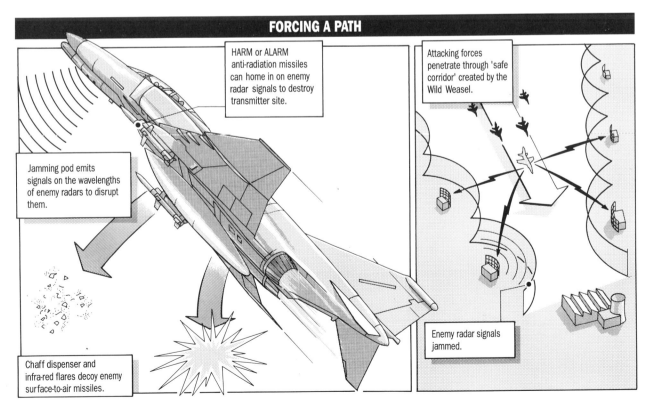

HARM or ALARM anti-radiation missiles can home in on enemy radar signals to destroy transmitter site.

Attacking forces penetrate through 'safe corridor' created by the Wild Weasel.

Jamming pod emits signals on the wavelengths of enemy radars to disrupt them.

Chaff dispenser and infra-red flares decoy enemy surface-to-air missiles.

Enemy radar signals jammed.

# INTERDICTION IN THE GULF WAR
## Rolling thunder that neutralized Iraq

**O**NE of the biggest problems confronting those responsible for planning the Allied air interdiction campaign against Iraq was to make an accurate intelligence assessment of Iraq's military capability.

The building of an overall intelligence picture had been largely left to the US Central Intelligence Agency, which relied heavily on intelligence provided by Israel. Since it was in Israel's own interests to paint as gloomy a picture as possible of Iraq's military capability, the end result was that Iraq's capability to wage a high-technology war was greatly over-estimated, and this affected the choice of targets and the method of attack in the early stages.

### PLANNING THE CAMPAIGN

The main priorities of the air interdiction phase of Desert Storm were to destroy Iraq's capacity to wage war with nuclear, chemical and biological weapons, to neutralize her Air Force's major airfields, and to disrupt the country's command, control and communication systems, to make them ineffective. This phase assumed the proportions of a strategic air war against industrial as well as military objectives.

The main weapons used against the command, control and communications system, whose primary sites were in built-up areas, were the Lockheed F-117A 'Stealth' aircraft of the 37th Tactical Fighter Wing and the General Dynamics AGM-109 Tomahawk Cruise missile, the latter launched from the battleships USS *Wisconsin* and USS *Missouri*. The F-117As were armed with laser-guided BLU-109 2,000 lb high explosive (HE) bombs, while the Cruise missiles were fitted with a 1,000 lb HE warhead.

More than 20 F-117As were deployed to Saudi Arabia and these bombed all their assigned targets on the first night of offensive operations. Pilots made good use of their aircraft's ability to remain undetected in the target area for lengthy periods while targets were verified. The pilots were also aided by the climate; the night on which the war began was clear and dark, with a new moon in its early phase. These are the best conditions for the night vision equipment used on Allied strike aircraft, and for the 'smart' weapons they carry. They are also ideal for Cruise missiles. The optical scanner that guides a Tomahawk can get confused under certain circumstances like fog, clouds, dust or smoke.

Other hard targets during the night interdiction phase were attacked by McDonnell Douglas F-15E Strike Eagles of the 336th Tactical Fighter Squadron, which forms part of the 4th Tactical Fighter Wing, and by US Navy Grumman A-6 Intruders, the latter operating from aircraft carriers in the Red Sea.

Tornados of the RAF, Royal Saudi Air Force and Italian Air Force were given the task of neutralizing

*A rarely-seen Lockheed F-117A 'Stealth' fighter streams its 'low-viz' parachute after returning from a bombing mission.*

① Missile is launched on high trajectory from ship or land.

② Cruise drops down for low-level flight over land, automatically checking its flight path by its unique terrain contour matching (TER[ sensors. The route is pre-mapped by sat[ and programmed to avoid enemy defence[

the Iraqi airfields. Some attacks were also made on petrol, oil and lubricant installations. The RAF Tornado GR1s made their airfield attacks using the JP233 Low Altitude Airfield Attack System, the technique being to make diagonal bomb-runs across runways, in order to isolate Iraqi aircraft in their hardened shelters. RAF Tornados carried the Sky Shadow ECM pod, and in some cases were also assisted by USAF Wild Weasel F-4Gs. The flight to

the target was made on autopilot, with the pilot taking over manually for the final pass at very low level, pulling the aircraft up a little during the run over the target to ensure the necessary clearance on weapons release and ready to take evasive action against SAM or anti-aircraft gunfire.

The Iraqi command, control and communications centres, fixed SS-1C Scud missile sites, nuclear reactors, chemical/biological warfare production and

*A Tornado GR1's JP233 Low Altitude Attack System in action. Tornado crews had a dangerous and difficult job of neutralizing Iraq's airfields.*

*The airfield component of the JP233 system is the Thorn EMI SG357. It is effective against roads, railways and bridges as well as airfields.*

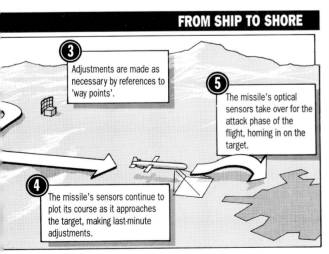

**FROM SHIP TO SHORE**

③ Adjustments are made as necessary by references to 'way points'.

⑤ The missile's optical sensors take over for the attack phase of the flight, homing in on the target.

④ The missile's sensors continue to plot its course as it approaches the target, making last-minute adjustments.

## LIGHTING THE WAY

Carried by the F-111F and used in conjunction with Paveway laser-guided bombs, the Pave Tack laser designating system is housed in a 13 ft streamlined pod. At the rear of this is the detecting set, rather like an infra-red TV camera with a zoom lens. The detecting set can be pointed in any direction by the F-111's Weapon System Officer (WSO) using a small hand controller, and provides him with a TV infra-red picture of the target. He then aligns the target in his sighting reticle in his cockpit, illuminates it with a laser and releases the bomb which rides down the reflected energy of laser. The photograph shows an actual TV image: the white blobs are tanks and the WSO is guiding the bomb directly onto one of them.

storage sites, rocket propellant plants, other military factories and airfields were all hit during this phase, although some suffered relatively minor damage. By the end of the first week of the air campaign, Iraqi radar activity had been reduced by 95 per cent, although this was partly due to deception and the re-deployment of mobile radar sites. Of 30 Iraqi main operating airfields, 25 had been heavily attacked by 23 January 1991, and the Iraqi Air Force's sortie rate had fallen from a daily average of over 200 before the onset of Desert Storm to about 40.

### THE SECOND PHASE

Once Iraq's capacity to wage strategic warfare had been eliminated, and total air supremacy had been achieved, the Allies were free to undertake the next phase of the campaign, the isolation by air attack of the Kuwait Operational Theatre. This was achieved by the systematic interdiction of roads, railways, indeed every means the Iraqis might employ to reinforce their army in Kuwait using all available air power, including USAF B-52s of Strategic Air Command.

Tornados, F-15Es and A-6s were now joined by F-111s and F-16s from bases in Turkey and Saudi Arabia, and by F/A-18 Hornets of the US Navy and Marine Corps, the whole operating under an escort fighter umbrella of USAF F-15C Eagles, USN F-14 Tomcats, and Canadian Armed Forces CF-18s. The latter, deployed from Germany, had the task of flying combat air patrols to protect the Allied fleet in the Gulf, and were based at Dhofar, Oman.

The General Dynamics F-111Fs involved in the interdiction campaign were mainly drawn from the 48th Tactical Fighter Wing, USAF, part of which was deployed to Incirlik in Turkey from RAF Lakenheath in Suffolk. In April 1986, the 48th TFW had participated in attacks on targets in Libya, when the United States took armed action in response to that nation's growing involvement with international terrorism.

The 48th TFW's F-111Fs are fitted with the Pave Tack laser designating system, which is housed in a streamlined pod under the aircraft's centre fuselage. This is used in conjunction with a typical weapon load of four 2,000 lb Paveway bombs, carried on underwing pylons. The system is extremely accurate against precision targets such as bridges - powerful enough in terms of explosive to bring down a strongly built structure of steel, masonry or concrete, and accurate enough to hit it in exactly the right place.

### F111F BOMBING TECHNIQUES

Bridges were primary targets for the F-111Fs in Iraq, and the 48th TFW achieved excellent results. The usual bombing attack technique employed was to approach the target at low altitude, then, at a pre-determined distance, pull up into a 4g climb and lob the bombs in the direction of the target several miles away. After bomb release the aircraft turned steeply through 90 degrees in a wing-over manoeuvre. The bombs were released at intervals of a fraction of a second to ensure separation and were initially aimed using radar. The Weapon Systems Operator (WSO) then held the Pave Tack designa-tor on the target throughout the flight of the bombs, guiding them down on the target until impact.

RAF Tornado GR1s, lacking their own laser-designator pod, operated alongside Buccaneers of the RAF Lossiemouth Strike Wing which were equipped with Pave Spike laser designator pods, the Buccaneer illuminating the target - often a hardened aircraft shelter, bridge or missile silo - and guiding the bombs after release by the Tornado. Two Tornados equipped with the GEC Ferranti TIALD (Thermal Imaging/ Airborne Laser Designator) were deployed to the Gulf and used operationally in interdiction attacks from 10 February.

TIALD is the only targeting pod to offer thermal imaging and TV as prime sensors. These can be selected in flight to provide 24-hour all-weather capability. This self-contained system had many advantages compared with tactics involving a dedicated laser-designator like the Buccaneer, flying as part of a group of aircraft carrying laser-guided bombs.

In one instance, a Tornado was lost when its crew, their heads down in the cockpit and with a lot of voice chatter in progress between the other aircraft in the group, failed to receive warning of a missile threat until it was too late. The Tornado was hit by two SA-3 missiles in rapid succession; the pilot ejected and was taken prisoner, but the navigator was killed. Such are the perils of interdiction.

### THE 48TH'S SCORE BOARD

Some 66 F-111Fs of the 48th Tactical Fighter Wing from RAF Lakenheath in England were deployed to the Gulf under Operation Desert Shield. When Desert Shield turned into Desert Storm the 48th TFW were in the forefront of the interdictor operations.

Their operational bombing record is impressive, as is the amount of money that literally fell from the aircraft - $94,835,671.15! Over 5,570 bombs were dropped, totalling 7.3 million lb in weight. The various kinds of bombs varied greatly according to the target: 410 were GBU-10s, 2542 GBU-12s, 212 were CBU-89s.

The targets themselves were tremendously varied. They ranged from 160 bridges , 9 towers, to 113 bunkers. There were 321 secondary explosions and 14 'miscellaneous' other targets.

Mission hours were long: 9,381 over a total of 2,417 sorties. All four squadrons took part, with the Wing commander's aircraft having flown the greatest number of individual missions. The aircraft clocked up 56 over the 42 days of the war.

*A close-up view of the underwing stores on the 48th TFW F-111F which flew the largest number of the 48th Tactical Fighter Wing's missions.*

# WEAPONS OF INTERDICTION From iron bomb to Tomahawk

**T**HE Allied air forces used a massive array of weaponry in their interdiction campaign against Iraq. They are the same weapons that at one time would have been used in a war between NATO and the Warsaw Pact. They ranged from simple iron General Purpose bombs to the sophisticated Cruise - and they showed an effectiveness that astonished even the most optimistic armament experts.

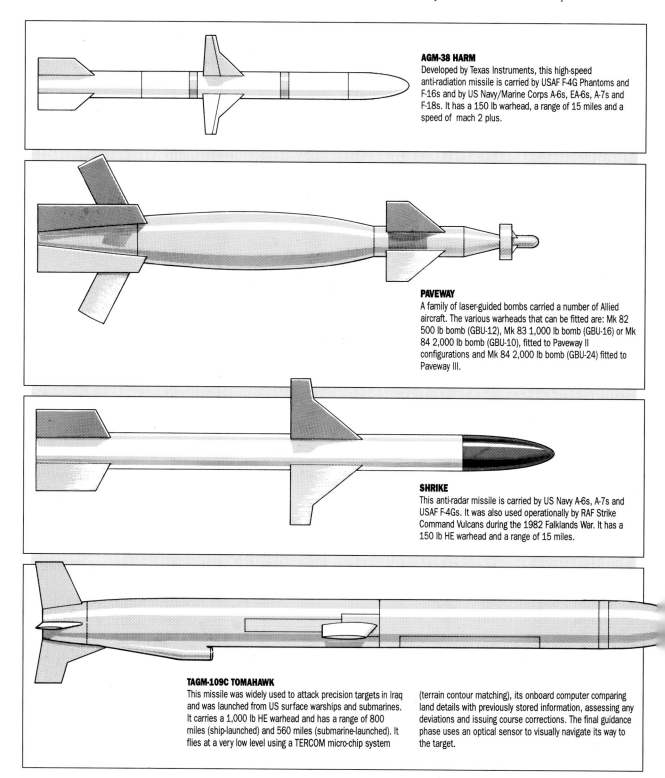

**AGM-38 HARM**
Developed by Texas Instruments, this high-speed anti-radiation missile is carried by USAF F-4G Phantoms and F-16s and by US Navy/Marine Corps A-6s, EA-6s, A-7s and F-18s. It has a 150 lb warhead, a range of 15 miles and a speed of mach 2 plus.

**PAVEWAY**
A family of laser-guided bombs carried a number of Allied aircraft. The various warheads that can be fitted are: Mk 82 500 lb bomb (GBU-12), Mk 83 1,000 lb bomb (GBU-16) or Mk 84 2,000 lb bomb (GBU-10), fitted to Paveway II configurations and Mk 84 2,000 lb bomb (GBU-24) fitted to Paveway III.

**SHRIKE**
This anti-radar missile is carried by US Navy A-6s, A-7s and USAF F-4Gs. It was also used operationally by RAF Strike Command Vulcans during the 1982 Falklands War. It has a 150 lb HE warhead and a range of 15 miles.

**TAGM-109C TOMAHAWK**
This missile was widely used to attack precision targets in Iraq and was launched from US surface warships and submarines. It carries a 1,000 lb HE warhead and has a range of 800 miles (ship-launched) and 560 miles (submarine-launched). It flies at a very low level using a TERCOM micro-chip system (terrain contour matching), its onboard computer comparing land details with previously stored information, assessing any deviations and issuing course corrections. The final guidance phase uses an optical sensor to visually navigate its way to the target.

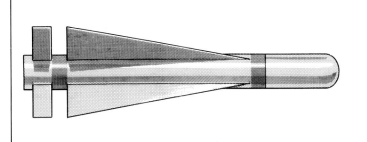

### AGM-65 MAVERICK
Although essentially a battlefield missile, Maverick can also be used on interdiction missions. It is compatible with a wide variety of aircraft weapons systems and is in service with over 200 air arms worldwide. The AGM-65A/B versions are TV-guided, the AGM-65D/F/G have an imaging infra-red guidance system, while the AGM-65s is laser guided. Weight of the warhead varies between 130 lb and 300 lb depending on the version, and range is 12 - 15 miles.

### AGM-130L
Developed by Rockwell International, the AGM-130 is in effect a rocket-boosted GBU-15 glide bomb and is carried mainly by USAF F-111s. It has an imaging infra-red guidance system and carries a 2,000 lb Mk 84 high explosive warhead. Its range is 16 miles.

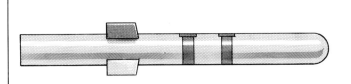

### DURANDAL
Developed by Matra, this French rocket-boosted runway-cratering bomb is carried by both French Air Force Jaguars as well as USAF F-15E Strike Eagles and F-111s. It was used operationally in Chad and Iraq. The whole weapon, including rocket motor, weighs 500 lb and it has a 34 lb warhead.

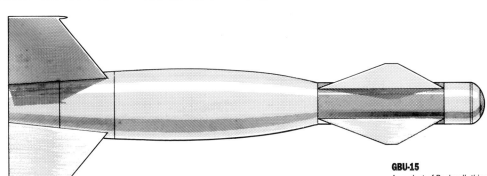

### GBU-15
A product of Rockwell, this glide bomb can be fitted with either a TV or infra-red imaging guidance system. It carries a 2,000 lb warhead comprising of a Mk 884 HE bomb, BLU-109 penetration bomb for use against hardened targets, or an SUU-54 submunitions dispenser. Its range varies between one and 50 miles, depending on the attack profile. The missile is carried by USAF F-111s, F-117s, F-15Es and SAC B-52s.

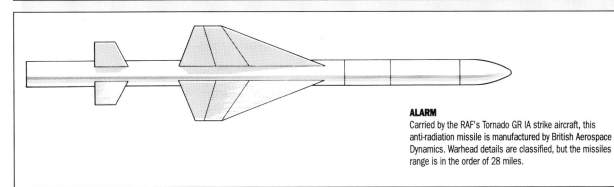

### ALARM
Carried by the RAF's Tornado GR IA strike aircraft, this anti-radiation missile is manufactured by British Aerospace Dynamics. Warhead details are classified, but the missiles range is in the order of 28 miles.

# CHAPTER THREE

# FORCE FROM THE AIR

IT was the Germans who, in 1918, were the first to produce dedicated ground-attack aircraft to provide battlefield support. In the closing months of the 1914-18 war, the German Flying Corps made widespread use of Schlachtstaffeln - literally, battle squadrons - whose aircraft carried extra armour and armament for the ground attack role.

In the Second World War, the Russians assumed the leadership in the design and operational use of heavily-armoured ground attack aircraft, the Ilyushin I1-2 Shturmovik, which played such a key part in the great tank battles of the Eastern Front, being the classic example.

Although Britain and America both produced experimental aircraft to fulfil the same role, in practice their tactical air forces were equipped with aircraft such as the P-47 Thunderbolt and the Hawker Typhoon, both of which began life as pure fighters and were later adapted as fighter-bombers.

Perhaps the most telling demonstration of tactical air power in the Second World War came in August 1944, when 50,000 German troops and all the heavy equipment of the Seventh and Fifth Panzer Armies were trapped in the Falaise Gap, Normandy, and systematically destroyed by the RAF 2nd and USAF 9th Tactical Air Forces.

There were similar effective demonstrations of tactical air power in the Korean War, when time and again a systematic air attack came to the rescue of United Nations forces in danger of being overrun by numerically superior enemy armies. The ground attack weapons used in that conflict were basically those of the Second World War - cannon, rockets, anti-personnel bombs and napalm - but the Korean War provided the basis for future generations of specialized ground attack weapons which, some years later, would be put to good use in Vietnam.

Tactical support in Normandy 1944. RAF ground crew re-arming a Spitfire.

One major lesson, learned in Korea and confirmed in Vietnam, was that jet aircraft, because of their high speed, do not make the best ground attack platforms. Much of the close support work in Korea was undertaken by an aircraft that had played a prominent role in the Second World War - the North American F-51 Mustang; in Vietnam, it was the piston-engined A-1 Skyraider that was resurrected to carry out a similar task.

But in the long run, it was the combat helicopter, equipped with increasingly sophisticated attack systems, and heavily-armed forward air control aircraft like the North American OV-10 Bronco, that dominated the Vietnamese battleground. At the same time, a USAF requirement for a new close support aircraft, initiated in 1967, led to the development of the Fairchild Republic A-10

Thunderbolt II, an aircraft designed specifically for anti-tank operation on NATO's Central Front. The British had a different answer to the problem of fixed-wing close support; the vertical/short take-off and landing (V/STOL) Harrier, an aircraft capable of operating from virtually anywhere as long as logistical support was available. The Harrier's capability was proven beyond all doubt in the Falklands War, and underlined the fact that the choice of this remarkable aircraft by the United States Marine Corps, despite initial misgivings in some American circles, had been the right one.

All these battlefield support systems were to come together in close co-operation during the Gulf War where, together with strike aircraft such as the Anglo-French Jaguar, they were to unleash the awful doom that descended on the Iraqi army of occupation in Kuwait.

*Above:* The combat helicopter came into its own in the battlefield support role in Vietnam. Here UH-1 Iroquois deploy infantry.

*Left:* Take-off from road, grass field, or aircraft carrier deck is no problem for a V/STOL aircraft. Here US Marine Corps AV-8B, the US-made version of the UK's Harrier II, jumps away from a German field.

# APACHE AND A-10S  A deadly combination

**O**N the night of 16/17 January 1991, several hours before the start of the Allied air offensive against Iraq, eight McDonnell Douglas AH-64 Apache helicopters of the US 101st Airborne Division flew northward at low level into the desert darkness. The helicopters were heavily laden with extra fuel tanks, Hellfire air-to-surface missiles, 70 mm rockets and 30 mm ammunition. Accompanying them, for navigational purposes, was a USAF special operations Sikorsky CH-53.

### THE LIGHTNING RAID
The Apaches' mission was to penetrate deep inside Iraq and destroy two key radar sites, opening a corridor for the Allied strike aircraft assigned to key targets in the Baghdad area.

The mission involved a round trip of 950 nautical miles, and was flawless. The Apaches split into two attack groups in the target area, popping up to 100 feet at the last moment to launch a total of 15 laser-guided Hellfires, all of which hit the two radar sites. The helicopter teams also launched 100 70 mm rockets and strafed the targets with 4,000 rounds of 30 mm ammunition before leaving the area. The strike had lasted less than two minutes.

On the return journey, the Apaches landed at a desert rendezvous to take on fuel pre-positioned there by a US Army CH-47 'Fat Cow' helicopter. This was a time consuming operation, and it was well into the following morning by the time the force headed for the Saudi Arabian border. En route, the CH-47, which was equipped with the ALQ-144 infra-red countermeasures system, detected an Iraqi SAM launch and took evasive action, using chaff and flares. The missile nevertheless homed in and blew away the helicopter's aft landing gear. Despite this damage, the CH-47 still managed to limp home safely. While still in Iraqi airspace the Apaches, accompanied by Blackhawk, Chinook and Kiowa helicopters which had been positioned forward as a backup force, attacked any targets that they could see. One Apache and one Blackhawk were lost to ground fire.

This remarkable operation, which lasted fifteen hours from start to finish, including the time spent on the ground, highlighted the amazing versatility of the AH-64A.

The Apache is a helicopter that has been described by its manufacturer as a 'total system for battle'. Originally designed by Hughes Helicopters, a subsidiary of McDonnell Douglas since 1984, the

*In a test-firing in the southern USA, an AH-64 fires off a Hellfire missile. The Apache can carry eight Hellfires, four on each side of its fuselage.*

Apache was built to survive in its main anti-armour role. It has comprehensive electronic counter-measures systems, engines with a low infra-red signature to confuse surface-to-air missiles, and an airframe and systems capable of surviving hits by bullets of up to 23 mm calibre.

The Apache carries a two-man crew, the pilot sitting above and behind the gunner/co-pilot. The helicopter's 'eyes' are the target acquisition/ designation sight (TADS) and pilot's night vision sensor (PNVS), which although separate systems, are interlinked with one another.

The Apache carries a 30 mm M230 Chain Gun mounted on a rotating turret under the nose. This weapon is normally directed by TADS, but can be controlled by either crew member using his helmet sight. The gun mounting is collapsible, as is the forward section of the fuselage. The airframe, landing gear and crew seats are designed to absorb crash energy, enabling the crew to survive a deceleration of up to 13 times the normal force of gravity.

For its primary anti-armour mission the Apache carries 816 Hellfires and 440 rounds of 30 mm ammunition. In the airmobile escort role, 'riding shotgun' to troop-carrying helicopters, the weapon load is 38 two-and-three-quarter-inch folding-fin rockets and 1,200 rounds of 30 mm ammunition.

*The strange-looking growth on the top of this Apache's rotor-mast is the radar pod of the Longbow integrated fire control radar and missile system, which adds to the ability of the helicopter to target armour at long distances. It is due to be fitted on US Army AH-64s in the mid-1990s.*

TADS night vision scanner.

Radar warning antenna.

Target acquistion and designation sights (TADS).

TADS daylight scanner, comprising TV and direct vision optics.

## THE INDIAN'S 'EYES'

TADS comprises a direct-view optical system scanning over a wide-field angle of 18 degrees, which is reduced to 4 degrees with magnification, a TV camera, a laser spot tracker and laser rangefinder/designator, all mounted in a rotating nose turret. Output from the TADS and PNVS, which is basically a forward-looking infra-red (FLIR) system mounted in its own turret above the nose, is fed to video display units in both cockpits and to each crew member's integrated helmet and display sight system (IHADSS). This torch-like unit is fitted to the 'bonedome', with a monocular lens for the right eye.

TADS is operated by the gunner/co-pilot, while the PNVS is primarily controlled by the pilot. Both systems can be used to acquire and designate targets, to steer weapons, or to pass sighting information from one cockpit to another. This highly developed system had teething problems in the Gulf due to heat and dust, but the results in the subsequent conflict vindicated this.

*The A-10 is often deployed very close to the front-lines and ready for any emergency. Here, during training, an A-10 uses a road as a make-shift runway.*

The helicopter is fitted with a range of radar and infra-red jamming systems, and is powered by two General Electric T700-GE-701 turboshaft engines.

## THE MUD MOVER

The A-10, like the Apache, was born of the Vietnam War, which revealed a serious lack of an aircraft designed specifically for ground attack and close support. The result was an aircraft of unusual appearance and quite remarkable ugliness, yet the real beauty of the A-10 is the way it is designed to fulfil its main mission. This aspect of its design around which everything revolves is its ability to carry the maximum firepower and continue to survive in a highly hostile environment.

The aircraft is very heavily armoured, the pilot sitting in a titanium 'bathtub', and the airframe has a built-in redundant structure policy, which means that the pilot can regain control even if large portions of the airframe are shot away. The A-10's built-in firepower is its massive GBU-8/A 30 mm seven-barrel rotary cannon, which is mounted on the

centreline under the forward fuselage. The gun fires up to 4,200 rounds per minute of armour-piercing ammunition with a non-radioactive uranium core for greater impact, and is quite capable of destroying a light tank or armoured personnel carrier. The aircraft also has eight underwing and three under-fuselage attachments for up to 16,000 lb of bombs, missiles, gun pods and jammer pods, and carries the Pave Penny laser system pod for target designation.

A-10s normally operate in two-ship flights, and each pair can cover a swathe of ground up to six miles wide. In practice, however, the best swathe width has been found to be two to three miles, so that an attack can quickly be mounted by the second aircraft once the first pilot has made his firing pass on the target. With uranium-core ammunition, an A-10 pilot can engage enemy armour at a range of between 4,000 and 6,000 ft; the gunsight is calibrated at the 4,000 ft range mark. This, coupled with the aircraft's turning circle of 4,000 ft, means that the A-10 can engage a target without having to pass over it. A one-second burst will place 70 rounds in the target area, and as a complete 360-degree turn takes no more than sixteen seconds two A-10s can bring continuous fire to bear.

The A-10's principal enemy is anti-aircraft artillery such as the Soviet-built ZSU 23/4, and to stand any chance of survival in a hostile environment dominated by this weapon, the A-10 pilot must fly at 100 ft or less and never remain straight and level for more than four seconds. Survivability also depends on close co-operation between the two A-10s; while one engages the target, the other stands off and attacks anti-aircraft installations with its Maverick TV-guided missiles, six of which are normally carried on triple launchers slung on pylons under its wings.

## TANK BUSTING TACTICS

If an A-10 is attacked by a hostile fighter, the standard tactic is to turn head-on towards the threat and use 'coarse rudder' - yawing the aircraft from side to side - to spray the attacker with 30 mm ammunition, a manoeuvre calculated to unnerve the enemy pilot.

During the Gulf War, Apaches and A-10s joined forces in a formidable combination to strike at armour, artillery and infantry bunkers in Kuwait, leaving RAF and French Air Force Jaguars, Free

Kuwaiti A-4 Skyhawks and US Navy/Marine Corps F-18 Hornets to attack supply dumps, communications and command centres. The combination of Apache and Hellfire missiles proved highly effective against some of the tougher bunker targets, and played its part in convincing the Iraqis of Allied supremacy.

On one occasion during the Gulf War, 480 Iraqis surrendered to a single Apache after the helicopter had destroyed two bunkers of a defensive complex with Hellfires, and the crew of a loudspeaker-

*The 'sharp-end' of the A-10 Thunderbolt II. This multi-barrelled cannon can fire a lethal load of lead at a rate of 70 rounds per second and can engage a tank or another AFV from a range of 6,000 feet.*

equipped UH-60 Blackhawks had warned the occupants of the other bunkers that they would suffer the same fate if they did not give themselves up.

# THE JUMP AND SHOOT JET   One stick control

**O**NE of the most versatile and potent weapon systems that took part in the air onslaught against the Iraqi army of occupation in Kuwait was the United States Marine Corps' AV-8B Harrier II, the V/STOL (Vertical/Short Take-off and Landing) aircraft developed jointly by McDonnell Douglas and British Aerospace.

The Harrier II is the latest - but, in all probability, not the last - chapter of a story that began in 1957, when Hawker Aircraft Ltd launched the concept of the P1127 V/STOL aircraft. The P1127 was designed around the Bristol BE53 vectored-thrust engine, the forerunner of the Rolls-Royce Pegasus. In this revolutionary turbofan, air from the fan and the low-pressure compressor is diverted to the front pair of vectoring nozzles, while the remaining engine thrust is directed through the rear pair of rotating nozzles.

A development of the P1127, the Kestrel, was evaluated in 1965 at RAF West Raynham by pilots of the RAF, US Air Force, Navy and Army, and the Federal German *Luftwaffe*. The aircraft was selected by the RAF and, named Harrier GR1, entered service on 1 April 1969. This, the world's first operational V/STOL aircraft, was followed by the GR1A and GR3, the latter having a nose-mounted laser rangefinder and an uprated Pegasus Mk 103.

In 1966 six Kestrels were sent to the USA for tri-service trials on land and sea under the designation XV-6A, and in 1969 the US Marine Corps received approval to buy the first of 102 aircraft, with the designation AV-8A.

American funding had played a key role in the development of the Harrier, and it was Vietnam, a land war requiring timely, fixed-wing close air support, that finally influenced the purchase decision.

In the words of one senior USMC officer: *'We could not afford, both in terms of initial cost or the impact on logistics, to buy enough conventional airplanes to keep them in the air all the time waiting to be called. We had to look for something we could park closer to the front lines. The Harrier seemed to be the answer, so we purchased three squadrons to prove the concept. The more we tested it, the more we knew it would work.'*

However, although the AV-8A Harrier was conceptually correct, the Marines needed an aircraft with more capacity. As a result, the AV-8B Harrier II

*An AV-8B of the US Marine Corps VMA-331 'Bumble-bees', makes a low-level pass over the desert carrying a load of 500 lb snakeye retarded bombs.*

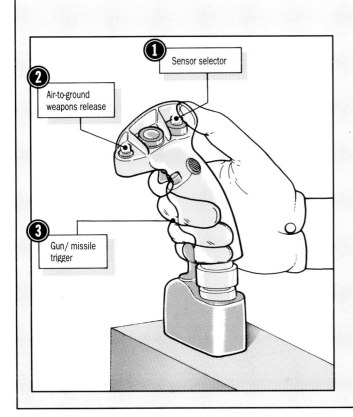

① Sensor selector

② Air-to-ground weapons release

③ Gun/ missile trigger

## ALL IN ONE HAND

In combat, pilots fly their aircraft with one hand on the stick and the other on the control column. The HOTAS concept, (HOTAS is simply 'Hands-on-throttle-and-stick'), means that it is no longer necessary for them to remove their hands to switch from one weapon or radar mode to another.

As the diagram shows, all the switches and buttons that are needed for armament or combat avionics are built either into the control column, or into the throttle, so that the pilot can alter his aircraft's combat configuration at the flick of a thumb.

The concept of locating all essential switchery on stick and throttle is by no means new. The system was incorporated from the outset in the General Dynamics F-16 Fighting Falcon, whose design began in 1972. In the F-16's case HOTAS was only one feature of an advanced cockpit designed to cut out errors while the aircraft performed very tight manoeuvres. The stick itself, mounted on the side of the cockpit, was given only a limited degree of movement to reduce manoeuvring errors at high g.

programme was launched. The design leadership of the advanced Harrier rested with McDonnell Douglas, but it soon developed into a joint effort between that company and British Aerospace, and it was to become the biggest Anglo-American collaborative aircraft programme in history.

### OVER TO THE USA

The Harrier II is fitted with the HOTAS (Hands-on Throttle-and-Stick) system, which allows the pilot, without letting go of either throttle or stick, to switch from an offensive to a defensive mode without taking his eyes from the enemy. *'So if I'm running in on target to destroy it and I'm being attacked, then with one flick of the thumb the Harrier II system completely changes all my sensors, arms my air-to-air weapons, changes my displays, head up and head down, and I am totally prepared for air combat. If the attacker doesn't turn in, then one more flick of my thumb and the aircraft goes back to being optimized for air-to-ground. In wartime, that's absolutely vital.'*

AV-8B pilots are very impressed by the Angle-Rate Bombing System, which is claimed to make the aircraft the most accurate air-to-ground weapons platform ever developed by the US Navy.

In the words of Lt Col James Cranford, who commanded Squadron VMA-331 at the time of its conversion to the AV-8B: *'The AV-8B is outstanding. On an A-4 or F-4 Squadron the old hands will achieve a CEP (Circular Error Probable - a measure of the accuracy attributable to ballistic weapons) of about 50 ft and the young guys will turn in 70-75 ft, something like that. And that's range work; in real life you've got SAMs, AAA, bad guys to contend with. With the AV-8B I can use terrain masking to run in low. My accurate inertial navigation system puts me on the Initial Point, I pull up and zoom, say to attack a SAM site, up high, roll in, drop on the SAMs before I get in range, then beat feet out of there. And do you know what's really nice? I won't have to go back and do it again tomorrow because I missed.'*

### A THIRD STEP IN THE FUTURE

In RAF service, the Harrier II is designated GR5 or GR7, the latter fitted with avionics to give it a night attack capability.

Development of this remarkable aircraft is ongoing; McDonnell Douglas and British Aerospace are now studying a 'Harrier III', an interim step towards a supersonic advanced short take-off/vertical landing (ASTOVL) aircraft for service early next century. The US Navy already has a requirement for such an aircraft, to be operational by 2010.

# DEFENDING THE BATTLEFIELD Mobile missiles and others

**G**ROUND attack pilots today have to contend with a formidable array of defensive weaponry, ranging from quick-firing small arms to radar-directed multi-barrel anti-aircraft artillery and guided missiles. All of it is highly mobile, in order to provide the necessary protection for fast-moving armoured and mechanized infantry units that are re-deployable at a moment's notice.

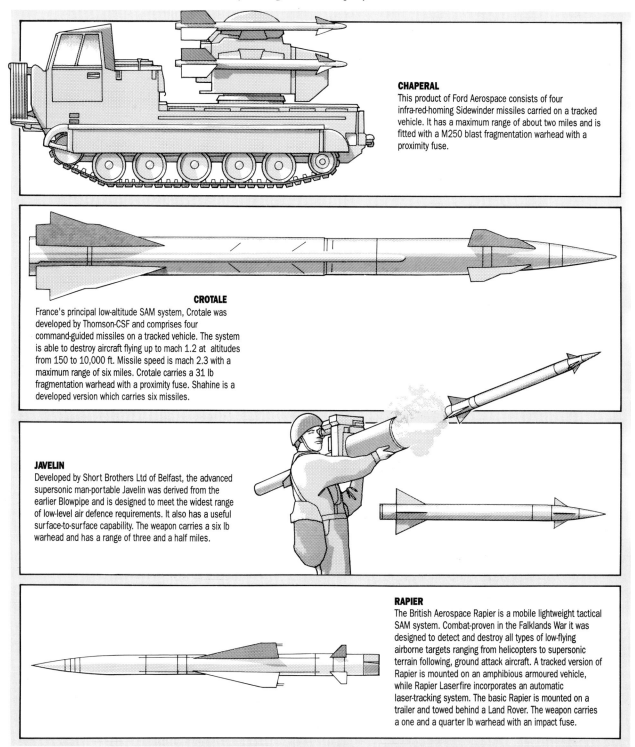

**CHAPERAL**
This product of Ford Aerospace consists of four infra-red-homing Sidewinder missiles carried on a tracked vehicle. It has a maximum range of about two miles and is fitted with a M250 blast fragmentation warhead with a proximity fuse.

**CROTALE**
France's principal low-altitude SAM system, Crotale was developed by Thomson-CSF and comprises four command-guided missiles on a tracked vehicle. The system is able to destroy aircraft flying up to mach 1.2 at altitudes from 150 to 10,000 ft. Missile speed is mach 2.3 with a maximum range of six miles. Crotale carries a 31 lb fragmentation warhead with a proximity fuse. Shahine is a developed version which carries six missiles.

**JAVELIN**
Developed by Short Brothers Ltd of Belfast, the advanced supersonic man-portable Javelin was derived from the earlier Blowpipe and is designed to meet the widest range of low-level air defence requirements. It also has a useful surface-to-surface capability. The weapon carries a six lb warhead and has a range of three and a half miles.

**RAPIER**
The British Aerospace Rapier is a mobile lightweight tactical SAM system. Combat-proven in the Falklands War it was designed to detect and destroy all types of low-flying airborne targets ranging from helicopters to supersonic terrain following, ground attack aircraft. A tracked version of Rapier is mounted on an amphibious armoured vehicle, while Rapier Laserfire incorporates an automatic laser-tracking system. The basic Rapier is mounted on a trailer and towed behind a Land Rover. The weapon carries a one and a quarter lb warhead with an impact fuse.

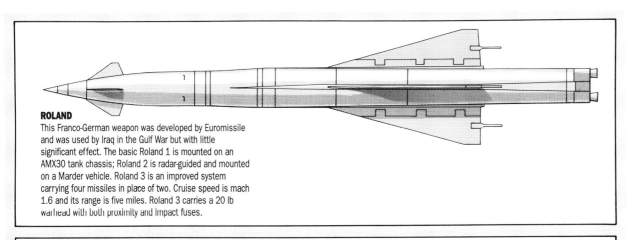

**ROLAND**
This Franco-German weapon was developed by Euromissile and was used by Iraq in the Gulf War but with little significant effect. The basic Roland 1 is mounted on an AMX30 tank chassis; Roland 2 is radar-guided and mounted on a Marder vehicle. Roland 3 is an improved system carrying four missiles in place of two. Cruise speed is mach 1.6 and its range is five miles. Roland 3 carries a 20 lb warhead with both proximity and impact fuses.

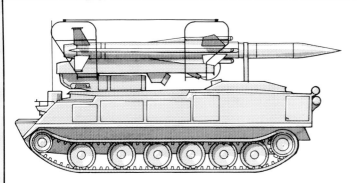

**SA-6 'GAINFUL'**
This Soviet SAM system is mounted on a PT-76 chassis, which carries three missiles. The weapon is boosted to a cruise speed of about mach 2.8 and carries a 126 lb warhead. It has a range of 15 miles. The SA-6 was used to devastating effect by Egypt in the 1973 Yom Kippur War, inflicting serious losses on Israeli strike aircraft.

**STINGER**
The United States is deficient in battlefield air defence systems, because of procurement and development caused by financial problems in the US Congress. However, it has an excellent man-portable SAM system in the form of the General Dynamics FIM-92 Stinger. This is a shoulder-launched infra-red missiles which can engage targets at a range of just under three miles. It carries a six and a quarter lb warhead.

In addition to the weapons mentioned above, the Soviet Union fields a whole family of battlefield missiles. The SA-7 'Grail', SA-14 'Gremlin', and the SA-16 are man-portable missiles, while the SA-8 'Gecko', SA-9 'Gaskin' and the SA-13 'Gopher' are all tracked or wheeled vehicles.

# CHAPTER FOUR

# EYES AND EARS OVER THE BATTLEFIELD

**A**LTHOUGH *the Chinese are thought to have made observations of enemy troop movements from man-lifting kites as long ago as the 12th century, the first recorded air reconnaissance flight took place on 26 June 1794 when two French officers, General Jourdan and Captain Coutelle, observed the course of the battle of Fleurus in Belgium from a tethered balloon. Reconnaissance balloons were used occasionally during the Napoleonic Wars and the American Civil War, but it was not until the Franco-Prussian War of 1870 that their use became widespread.*

*The military use of aircraft during the First World War revolutionized air reconnaissance techniques. The Royal Flying Corps, in particular, developed a very efficient air reconnaissance and army co-operation system,*

Air reconnaissance, 1917: an RE8 observation aircraft. Such machines suffered heavy losses photographing enemy trench positions.

*especially with regard to artillery spotting. Yet, between the wars, the British allowed both air reconnaissance and army co-operation to slide into a backwater, the RAF's emphasis being on the supremacy of the strategic bomber. It was not until after the outbreak of the Second World War that the RAF formed its first specialist*

'Before-and-after' views of the German research establishment at Peenamund, taken from RAF PR Spitfires.

'photo-recce unit', equipped with stripped-down, high-flying Spitfires and, later, with Mosquitos.

The German Luftwaffe had specialist photo-reconnaissance units from the outset, as did the Japanese. The Imperial Japanese Navy's 3rd Air Corps photographed strategic targets in the south-west Pacific long before the attack on Pearl Harbor. The Germans continued to develop specialist reconnaissance aircraft until the final months of the war; the Junkers Ju 86P, for example, could reach altitudes of over 40,000 feet, while from July 1944 until Germany's collapse, Arado Ar 234 jet reconnaissance aircraft were operating with impunity over the British Isles from bases in France, and later, Norway.

The beginning of the so-called Cold War in the late 1940s brought about a requirement for a truly long-range strategic reconnaissance aircraft - one that could overfly the Soviet Union while operating from advanced bases in the British Isles, or even from the United States itself. The requirement was filled by a specially-adapted version of Strategic Air Command's mighty B-36 bomber, the RB-36D. The aircraft's bomb-bay was turned into a pressurized compartment crammed with photographic and surveillance equipment, including some capable of monitoring radioactive debris from Soviet nuclear tests. The RB-36D's role was later taken over by the XB-47 Stratojet.

In 1956, a new and mysterious aircraft made its appearance in the skies of the United States and Europe. Named the Lockheed U-2, the official stance was that it was a weather observation aircraft. Its true role became clear on 1 May 1960, when one was shot down by a missile battery near Sverdlovsk, deep inside the Soviet Union.

Soviet missile technology had caught up with the U-2, a fact underlined in successive years when more were lost during overflights of Communist China and Cuba. What was needed now was a strategic reconnaissance aircraft that could not only outrange hostile missiles, but also outrun them. In 1964, USAF Strategic Air Command began to take delivery of such an aircraft, the Lockheed SR-71 Blackbird. A truly remarkable aircraft, years ahead of its time in terms of technology, the Blackbird was capable of flying 3,000 miles at a speed of Mach 3 and an altitude of 80,000 ft. Fitted with powerful countermeasures systems, it remained capable of out-performing every type of Soviet-designed surface-to-air missile system for twenty years.

By then, satellite reconnaissance systems had reached such an advanced state that the requirement for a manned strategic reconnaissance aircraft had passed, although tactical recce of aircraft were still a vital necessity. The overall surveillance of the battlefield, and the airborne direction of the forces , were now the key factors.

The Lockheed SR-71A Blackbird, the most advanced strategic 'recce' aircraft of all time. Its role has now been assumed by satellites.

# EYES OF THE STORM The constant watch from space

**A**T the height of the Gulf War, no fewer than fourteen US reconnaissance and intelligence-gathering satellite systems were deployed in support of Operation Desert Shield, the build-up phase prior to the launching of the Allied offensive, Desert Storm, against Iraq. These systems fell into three broad categories: optical reconnaissance, radar surveillance and signals intelligence. The latter category is sub-divided into electronic intelligence (ELINT) and communications intelligence.

The most important system in the first category was the KH-11 'Key Hole' optical imaging satellite, two of which were deployed in support of the Gulf operations. Developed jointly by the US Air Force and the Central Intelligence Agency, the first Key Hole satellite was launched in December 1976 and the system has been constantly updated and refined since then. Key Hole is, in effect, a military version of the Hubble Space Telescope, with a length of 64 ft and a diameter of 6 and a half ft. It can remain in orbit for two years, following an elliptical path varying between 185 and 275 miles above the earth.

Data and pictures from its sensors are transmitted to ground stations in digital form, and in good conditions its high-resolution cameras can detect objects the size of a grapefruit on the ground. It is also equipped with infra-red cameras that can detect heat emissions from missiles, aircraft and vehicles.

### STATE OF THE ART SKY SPIES

Two even more advanced KH-12 satellites were also diverted to support Desert Shield, something that would not have been possible before the end of the Cold War. The main task of KH-11 and KH-12 was to provide constant photographic coverage of Soviet military installations.

In the second category, the principal radar reconnaissance satellite system was 'Lacrosse', which was first launched in 1988 and which follows a similar type of orbit to Key Hole. Lacrosse carries a synthetic-aperture radar system which enables it to scan the earth's surface by day, night and in all weathers, even through clouds. The lens can resolve objects three feet across. The reflected radar waves are analysed by the satellite's on-board equipment, and the information passed to ground stations on earth by relay satellites.

Two main satellite systems were used in the signals intelligence-gathering role. These were Magnum and

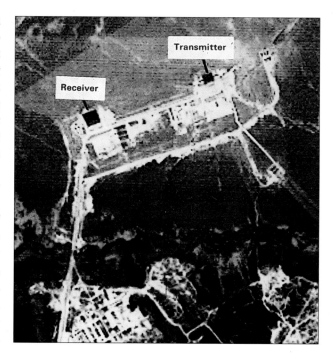

*The Pechora Large Array radar Transmitter system in the USSR is caught on this satellite image. Classified images contain much more detail than this one.*

Chalet, the former launched by the Space Shuttle and the latter by a Titan 34D booster. The task of both sytems was to monitor 'walkie-talkie', telephone and radio, radar, microwave and telemetry

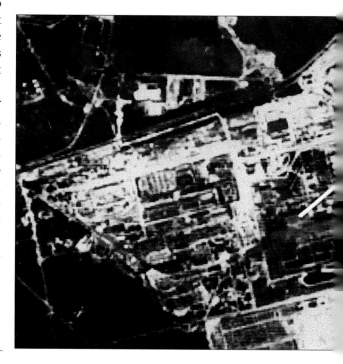

## THE WATCH FROM SPACE

Relay satellite processes data beamed to it by ELINT satellites and re-transmits it to control stations on earth.

Electronic intelligence (ELINT) satellites such as the top secret US Whitecloud, in geostationary orbit 22,500 miles above the earth, intercept and record electronic activity which is then sent back to earth via relay satellite.

Photographic reconnaissance satellite like the KH-11 Keyhole orbits at between 180 and 300 miles and relays high-resolution optical and infra-red images to earth. It can distinguish objects the size of a grapefruit.

transmissions from geostationary orbits 22,500 miles above the earth. The signals were 'dumped' to the Pine Gap receiving station in Australia, and then re-transmitted via communications satellites to other ground stations.

### SCUD SPOTTER

One vital function in the Gulf War was performed by another geostationary satellite system called DPS (Defence Programme Support) 14. Launched in November 1990, its task was to provide early warning of Iraqi missile launches. It is fitted with a

powerful infra-red telescope, operating in two wavelengths to avoid laser jamming.

The telescope detects rocket exhaust plumes against the Earth's background. During surveillance of Iraq, images were transmitted constantly to the USAF tracking station at Alice Springs and routed via several communications links to the Missile Early Warning Center at NORAD, Colorado; the information was also passed to ground terminals in Saudi Arabia, alerting Patriot missile batteries to the threat of incoming Scuds.

It was DPS 14 that gave the Patriot battery commanders the warning time they needed; without it, their success rate might have been much lower.

The vital military role played by reconnaissance satellites would make them high-value targets in any war between the major powers. The destruction of an enemy's satellite system would leave him blinded and open to surprise attack. Indeed, the preliminary report made by the Department of Defence after the Gulf War touched on the vital question of the vulnerability of satellite links. Because of the shortage of ground receiving equipment issued to the troops in the field, it was necessary to use commercially available equipment and not to encrypt the transmissions. Those transmissions could have been jammed by Saddam Hussein with dire consequences for the Allies.

*The Chernobyl reactor explosion in the USSR was first noticed on military satellite surveillance photographs.*

Reactor No 4

# AWACS AND TR1 Controlling the battle

WHILE satellite reconnaissance information was essential to the building up of an overall strategic picture of events in the Gulf, the tactical control and direction of the war was the responsibility of two main airborne systems, the Boeing E-3 Sentry Airborne Warning and Control System (AWACS) and the Lockheed TR-1A battlefield surveillance aircraft.

The Boeing E-3, originally known as the EC-137, stems from a NATO need for an early warning aircraft equipped with radar systems capable of extending the low-altitude radar view of Warsaw Pact territory by as much as 150 miles, thereby filling the existing gaps in low-altitude coverage left by ground-based radars, and providing a major advance in early warning protection.

The aircraft's role was summed up by General John S. Pustay, Director of the USAF AWACS Task Force, speaking in 1976, a year before the first E-3As entered USAF service:

'The E-3A would not only be able to track enemy formations as they approach the border; it would also make very difficult the deceptive forward assembly of large numbers of aircraft. Through routine surveillance...we could monitor typical aircraft activity patterns throughout East Germany and the western portions of Czechoslovakia and Poland. We could then determine changes in patterns which may be threatening - not only an obvious infusion of attack aircraft at forward bases,...but more subtle activities such as the movement of support and transport aircraft out of the forward zone to clear ramp and hangar space to an unusual degree.

Acting on such changes in pattern, or whenever our intelligence suggests a need for more concentrated surveillance, we could deploy more E-3As and fly continuous orbits to provide uninterrupted surveillance.'

## A FADING STAR IN THE EAST

Although the threat from eastern Europe has receded, if not entirely vanished, the core of the E-3's role today, together with the direction of fighter aircraft, remains to stop an airborne threat. Its primary function in the Gulf War was to detect the movement of Iraqi aircraft and to direct Allied fighters to the point where a successful interception could be made.

At the heart of the E-3's systems is its Westinghouse surveillance radar, which in its latest version can track targets more than 200 nautical miles away while cruising at 30,000 ft. The 30 ft diameter radome turns at six revolutions per minute when the equipment is active, and has various operating modes depending on the task in hand. The standard E-3A's radar was later modified to track ships, and other modifications included the fitting of a faster central computer with expanded memory, together with improved communications equipment. This included the Joint Tactical Information Distribution System (JTIDS), which ensures an unbroken transmission of data if main communications links are disrupted.

## EARLY STEALTH IN OPERATION

Developed from the earlier Lockheed U-2, the TR-1A has the task of providing day and night all-weather surveillance of the battle area. It is a key element in the support of US and Allied ground troops and air forces during times of crisis and war.

Roughly half the total force of 29 aircraft, which are deployed at various locations throughout the world under the command of the 17th Strategic Reconnaissance Wing, are equipped with the

Left and opposite: *This E-3A Sentry is coming into land after a routine mission. The large radar housing can clearly been seen and makes this aircraft unmistakable to identify. Its interior is crammed with monitoring equipment.*

## THE VIEW FROM ON HIGH

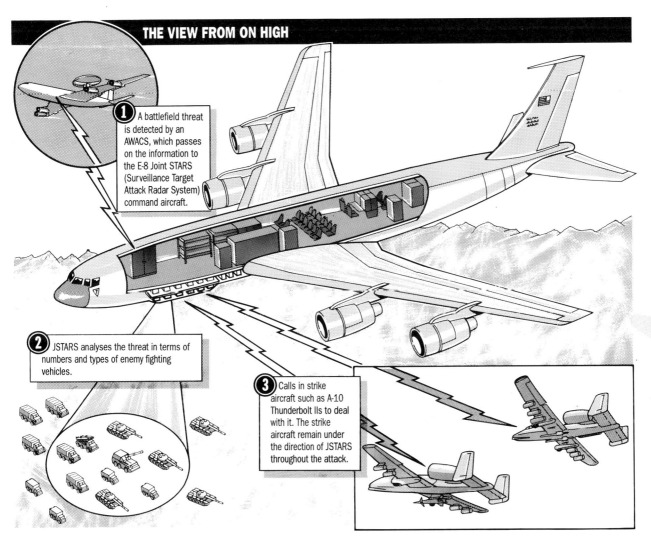

**1** A battlefield threat is detected by an AWACS, which passes on the information to the E-8 Joint STARS (Surveillance Target Attack Radar System) command aircraft.

**2** JSTARS analyses the threat in terms of numbers and types of enemy fighting vehicles.

**3** Calls in strike aircraft such as A-10 Thunderbolt IIs to deal with it. The strike aircraft remain under the direction of JSTARS throughout the attack.

Precision Location/Strike System (PLSS), enabling them to detect and locate enemy emitters and direct strike aircraft on to them. In carrying out its task the TR-1A slowly circles at up to 90,000 ft, from which altitude its highly secret sensors can 'see' many miles into hostile territory.

The Gulf War saw the first operational use of the Boeing E-8 JSTARS (Joint Surveillance Target Attack Radar System) aircraft. Developed from the Boeing 707 airliner, the E-8 carries very advanced surveillance systems to detect second-echelon ground concentrations deep behind enemy lines. The aircraft's computers then broadcast target information to both ground and air forces: directing in tactical and strike aircraft, missile strikes or artillery as needed.

JSTARS was rushed into service in the Gulf well before it had completed its allotted test programme. However, its presence undoubtedly helped in the enormous task of directing the flights of thousands of aircraft and the movements of troops every day in the theatre of war.

# DRONES AND REAL-TIME RECONNAISSANCE
## Painting the battlefield picture

**D**RONES, unmanned aircraft properly called remotely piloted vehicles (RPVs), have been used for reconnaissance for many years. Some were developed from target drones, used to train anti-aircraft gunners and missile operators. One such was the Teledyne Ryan BQM-34A, a turbojet-powered target drone which, in the 1960s, was fitted with reconnaissance cameras and air-launched by a Lockheed C-130 Hercules to make overflights of China and North Vietnam.

Israel is one of the principal exponents of RPV technology. Drones developed by the Malat Division of Israeli Aircraft Industries were used extensively on combat missions against Syrian forces in Lebanon in the 1980s. The main RPV employed in these operations was the Scout, a high-wing design with twin tail booms. The Scout carries a recon-naissance payload of 70 lb and is powered by a two-stroke 'pusher' piston engine.

### SCOUTS OVER LEBANON

The Scout is controlled by a ground control station (GCS) which receives, computes and displays real-time data from the RPV, including a TV picture of the target area, via an automatic tracking antenna and a two-way data link. The control station can send back messages to the RPV and control its movements via the same highspeed data link.

The GCS is manned by a crew of four: mission officer, operator, payload operator and technician, working in the comfort of an air-conditioned shelter.

With a wingspan of only 12 feet, the Scout is undetectable above 3,000 ft. Its wing, booms and tail, made up from composite materials, render it almost invisible to radar, while its piston engine produces a very small infra-red signature compared with a jet-powered RPV. The Scout, operating over the Bekaa Valley, transmitted its TV data instantaneously and its effectiveness was ably demonstrated in a notable series of air strikes that took place on 9 June 1982 against Syrian SAM sites in Lebanon. During these operations, drones were used both for reconnaissance and as decoys, and the data they transmitted to the GCS led to the destruction of the SAM sites by F-4 Phantoms, equipped with Maverick and Shrike missiles, and by short-range surface-to-surface missiles.

Scout drones were also used to pinpoint targets in Beirut, to monitor terrorist movements and to keep track of Syrian tank forces. The RPV, which has an an operational flight-time of seven hours, was also used to monitor the evacuation by ship of the Palestine Liberation Organisation.

The transmission of data instantaneously, or in 'real time' as it is known, proved particularly useful to the Israeli ground forces, who no longer had to rely on conventional reconnaissance photographs that took time to develop. The RPV's operations had considerable impact on the effective use of artillery. Previously, Israeli battery commanders needed up to ten minutes to correct their firing accuracy, whereas the Scout provided batteries with almost instant corrections based on the first shell burst.

As a result, artillery commanders found that their guns required loading at a faster rate. However, fewer shells were required, easing the logistics of keeping the guns supplied. The RPV also enabled commanders to see when their targets had been destroyed, rather than relying on calculation.

Israeli-built reconnaissance drones were also used extensively in the Gulf War. One system, the Pioneer, had in fact been operational for some time on board the battleships USS *Iowa* and USS *New*

*The MBB Tucan short-ramp launched drone is seen here in high-visibility markings used for trials. Usually drones are camouflaged.*

*Jersey*, and had been used to monitor events in the Gulf during the last year of the Iran-Iraq war.

In the more recent conflict, the RPVs were used to pinpoint Iraqi installations in Kuwait, building up an accurate intelligence picture that was used to good effect by Allied strike aircraft.

For some time, the US Air Force and US Navy have been working on a solution to the problem of providing tactical commanders with a real-time reconnaissance capability. The concept, known as the Advanced Tactical Air Reconnaissance System, involves both manned aircraft and RPVs. The new system will replace conventional photo-recon-naissance technology with advanced electro-optical sensors for low- and medium-altitude operations, together with an infra-red linescanner. The information collected will be passed through a digital recorder, and near-real-time capability will be achieved through a high-speed datalink.

ATARS is intended for use by existing tactical reconnaissance aircraft such as the RF-4C Phantom, and systems still under development, like the RF-18D Hornet for the US Marine Corps and the US Navy's F-14D(R) Tomcat.

It will also form the basis of equipment for a programme known as the Follow-on Tactical Reconnaissance System; this requirement will probably be met by a reconnaissance version of the General Dynamics Fighting Falcon, the RF-16.

Above and below: *The Heron-26/Mizar UAV is an experimental USAF drone. Seen here operating above the Mojave Desert, USA, the interior of the control room shows the banks of real-time images received from the drone .*

*The Mirach 26 RPV is a European drone system made by the Italian aerospace consortium Aeritalia. Like its Canadian counterpart it is trailer-launched.*

## CANADA'S CONTRIBUTION

Several of America's NATO partners, including the United Kingdom, use RPVs manufactured by the Canadian company Canadair. One of these, the CL-89, carries a Zeiss camera system and is powered by a turbojet engine. It flies at nearly 500 mph and has a range of 75 miles. An improved version, the CL-289, is launched from a truck, flies a pre-programmed flight path, records information and returns to base for recovery by parachute.

Another Canadair RPV system is the CL-227 Sentinel battlefield surveillance and target acquisition system. It uses a small rotary-wing RPV powered by a gas turbine engine driving two contra-rotating horizontal rotors. Sentinel can hover, and can reach a forward speed of 80 mph. It has an endurance of over three hours, and carries a payload of up to 100 lb.

## INTO THE NEXT CENTURY

In future wars, RPVs are likely to have far more than just a reconnaissance role. For example, the German firm Messerschmitt-Bolkow-Blohm had been carrying out development studies of an anti-tank RPV called the *Panzer Abwehr Drohne* (PAD), which is equipped with acoustic and millimetre-wave sensors. It is designed to work in conjunction with another projected RPV, named the *Kleinfluggerat Zielortung* (KZO) which is a drone capable of day and night, all-weather operation at ranges of about 30 miles from its launch point. Cruising at 140 mph and with a three-hour endurance, the KZO will use its infra-red, TV and laser sensors to detect enemy tanks, and then guide a PAD to the area. The PAD's acoustic sensor picks up the noise of the tank engines, and the RPV homes on to one of them, fine tuning its own course by using the sensors it carries in its body.

In the era of 'stealth' the use of drones has a high priority in defence circles. They are a cheap and viable alternative to manned aircraft. Basic 'stealth' technology can be found in ideas that have come from the research and development involved with RPVs. One, the USA's D-21, is known to have a top speed of Mach 4 and the technology is used in the SR-71.

*A Canadair CL-289 drone system is launched from its trailer in Germany. The system has been sold to France for delivery in the early 1990s.*

# CHAPTER FIVE

# DECEPTION AND DISGUISE

**T**HE *science of what is nowadays called electronic countermeasures (ECM) had its beginnings in the late 1930s, when the Germans used commercial aircraft and the airship* Graf Zeppelin *to photograph the radar masts that were springing up along Britain's coasts. This intelligence was later used to plan attacks on the radar installations during the Battle of Britain.*

*The first airborne countermeasures operations, though, took place in late 1940, when specially equipped RAF aircraft set out to discover how the Germans were able to bomb British cities such as Coventry with great accuracy, at night and in cloudy conditions. The RAF found that the Germans were using navigational radio beams, which intersected over the target and signalled the Luftwaffe crews when to release their bombs.*

*British signals specialists learned how to disrupt the beams and throw the bombers off course; the Germans retaliated with more advanced equipment that proved more difficult to jam. The countermeasures war was on.*

*The most significant ECM development of the Second World War was the invention of 'Window', strips of tinfoil cut to the wavelengths of enemy warning radar and dropped in bundles from attacking aircraft to confuse the enemy's defences. It was used operationally for the first time in July 1943, with disastrous consequences for the city of Hamburg. In November that year, the RAF formed No 100 (Countermeasures) Group. Bearing the apt motto 'Confound and Destroy', its task was to support night bombing operations by jamming German electronic defences and hunting enemy night-fighters. Its Mosquito and Beaufighter aircraft were equipped with a device called 'Serrate', which enabled them to home in onto German airborne radar transmissions.*

*American B-17 Flying Fortress aircraft were obtained and modified for the radar jamming role. They equipped No 214 Squadron and operated in conjunction with the USAF's 803rd Squadron, which was also controlled by No 100 Group. The Fortresses carried three main types of jamming equipment: 'Mandrel', which jammed ground radars, 'Piperack', which disrupted airborne interception radars, and 'Jostle', a noise-jamming device which blocked the German fighter control frequencies. All ECM equipment in use today stems, in principle, from these early devices.*

*The development of ECM in the Second World War also encompassed self-defence measures. In 1944, RAF night bombers were fitted with a radar warning instrument code-named 'Monica', which picked up transmissions from an approaching night-fighter's radar. This was the forerunner of today's radar warning receivers.*

Secret War: The Lichenstein airborne interception radar installation in a Junkers Ju 88 night fighter.

Perhaps the most convincing demonstration of ECM in the Second World War was Operation 'Taxable'. This was a mission carried out by eight Lancasters of No 617 Squadron in the early hours of 6 June 1944, as the Allied invasion fleet was heading for the Normandy beaches. The Lancasters formed up in two lines over the English Channel, each consisting of four aircraft abreast with four miles between each and a distance of eight miles between the lines. The Lancasters flew a series of 30 orbits, each describing an oblong eight miles by two, and each orbit was a mile ahead of the previous one to simulate a surface force moving across the Channel at a speed of about seven knots. On each of the eight-mile legs the Lancasters dropped 12 bundles of 'Window' per minute.

The whole operation was designed to simulate, on German radar, a huge invasion force heading for a completely different part of the French Channel coastline, and it worked. The Panzer divisions that might have destroyed the actual invasion were held in reserve to meet a non-existent threat, and when they finally moved towards the Normandy beach-heads the Allies were firmly ashore. The rest of the story is history.

In more recent years, Avro Vulcan jet bombers - the mainstay of Britain's nuclear deterrent force until 1969 - gave several effective demonstrations of ECM jamming during air exercises. On one occasion, in October 1961, eight Vulcans - four from No 27 Squadron and four from No 83 - were invited to take part in Exercise Skyshield, devised to test the efficiency of America's recently updated air defences. The Vulcans, using their full ECM capability during the exercise, penetrated the US defences at 56,000 feet without once being intercepted.

The Vulcan's ECM equipment was contained in a tail extension, seen here on an aircraft of No 35 Squadron.

# THE BLACK BOX Electronics at its most secret

**B**ECAUSE the effective use of electronic counter-measures is a key recipe for survival in modern air warfare, the subject is one of the most classified areas of military technology outside nuclear, chemical and biological weaponry. The longer it takes a potential enemy to guess what sort of ECM equipment lies inside the innocent-looking pods carried by combat aircraft, the longer it will take him to devise effective electronic counter-counter-measures (ECCM).

Before the crew of a combat aircraft can use their ECM equipment, they must first of all be aware that they are being scanned by hostile radar. Detecting this threat is the job of the aircraft's radar warning receiver (RWR). Because of the vast number of radar systems in current use, the RWR must be capable of processing and analysing the signals it receives, checking them against a library of radar signatures in the aircraft's computer memory and rejecting those which do not represent a threat.

In the early stages of an attack the main threat comes from long-range surveillance radars, which provide the necessary information for the enemy to prepare his defences, but closer to the target the threat switches to defensive systems which are attempting to track the attacking aircraft and guide missiles.

Some radar warning receivers directly control the aircraft's ECM systems, deploying chaff (the modern equivalent of the wartime 'Window' or flares, the latter to confuse heat-seeking missiles, as well as switching the aircraft's jamming equipment on and off. Jamming systems often incorporate receivers which continue to observe hostile transmissions during deliberate but brief gaps in the jamming, to assess the effectiveness of the techniques being used and to ensure that changes of radar frequency are noticed and promptly countered.

Ultra-modern ECM suites also incorporate laser warning receivers (LWR) which can be interfaced with other threat warning systems. Laser tracking systems, especially those combined with short-range SAM systems such as the British Aerospace Rapier, will be a dominant feature of tomorrow's battlefield.

### 'BARRAGE' AND 'SWEPT-SPOT'

One of the simplest methods of degrading radar performance is through noise jamming. Radar signals lose a lot of energy in the process of travelling to, and reflecting from, the target, so it is a relatively simple matter to drown them out with artificially created noise. Some noise jammers are set to transmit on the single frequency used by the hostile radar, while others spread their energy out over a band of frequencies. This is known as barrage jamming. Its disadvantage is that the jammer output is spread out along the spectrum instead of being concentrated on the actual operating frequency, so that in a 'one-against-one' engagement most of the energy is wasted. The other method, called spot jamming, involves knowing the exact enemy operating frequency before the start of a mission, or alternatively using a receiver and signal processor to detect the signal, and then tuning the jammer to its

*The business end of a EC-130A 'Compass Call' used alongside the 'Raven' for airborne heavyweight electrical jamming.*

## SENSING AND JAMMING

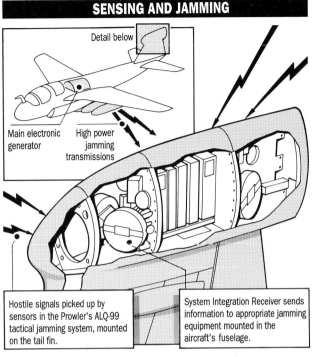

Detail below

Main electronic generator

High power jamming transmissions

Hostile signals picked up by sensors in the Prowler's ALQ-99 tactical jamming system, mounted on the tail fin.

System Integration Receiver sends information to appropriate jamming equipment mounted in the aircraft's fuselage.

*An EF-111A returns to base from its mission where it jammed and overloaded the enemy radars. During the Gulf War the EF-111As were constantly airborne, often working alongside the US Navy's Prowler ECM aircraft.*

*The British Aerospace Rapier defence system was widely used during the Gulf War for airfield defence. The weapon is often interfaced with ECM equipment.*

frequency. Another well used technique is swept-spot jamming, in which the jammer operating frequency scans through a band of enemy radar frequencies.

The most widely used ECM technique today is deception jamming, which provides hostile radar with false data. The technique involves receiving the signal from the radar, processing it in some way, then re-transmitting it in an attempt to persuade the radar to accept the spurious signal and derive false range and bearing information from it. The technique can have a disastrous effect on the automatic signal-processing circuitry in a radar, causing the antenna to lose its lock on the target. As soon as the target is re-acquired the ECM system promptly repeats the trick.

False target generation techniques can be used to create artificial returns on the hostile radar screen - signals which maintain tracks, manoeuvre and behave in every way like genuine targets. Used ruthlessly - as they were in the Gulf War by the USAF's EF-111 Raven and US Navy's EA-6B Prowler electronic warfare aircraft - such techniques can completely overload the radar display, filling the screen with so many false targets that they merge into a continuous signal and make it impossible for an enemy to work out any possible counter measure.

# THE BLACK BOX UPDATED
## The continuing research for electronic excellence

**B**ECAUSE defence systems are being upgraded and improved all the time, there is a constant need to update existing ECM suites installed in combat aircraft. Perhaps the best example of this ongoing requirement is provided by the Boeing B-52, an aircraft which has been in the front line of the USAF Strategic Air Command's nuclear strike force since 1955.

### HIGH POINT FOR THE B-52

The Vietnam War, in which 18 B-52s were destroyed by SA-2 Guideline SAMs during operations over the north, revealed the need for a radical update of the bomber's ECM suite. No fewer than fifteen of the B-52s were lost during 'Linebacker II', an 11-day series of bombing operations against targets in the Hanoi and Haiphong areas. The plan called for the B-52s to attack at night, in three waves, with F-111s and A-6s continuing the offensive in daylight. The B-52 bomber streams were preceded by F-111 interdictors, attacking fighter bases at low level, and by F-4 Phantoms dropping chaff. The B-52s approached their target areas from the north-west, using strong high-altitude winds to give them a much increased ground speed, and after bomb release they swung away from the targets in tight turns to clear the SAM defences as quickly as possible.

The attacks were made by cells of three aircraft, generally bombing from 33,000 ft. The three aircraft flew in close formation in order to pool their ECM resources, which included the General Electric ALQ-87 and ITT ALQ-117 radar jammers and the Lundy ALE-24 chaff dispensing system. In fact, the B-52Ds that bore the brunt of the bombing campaign were better equipped with ECM than the later-model B-52Gs, which were also brought in to augment the bombing force during Linebacker II.

As a result of the losses sustained during this operation - some of which, admittedly, occurred when unexpectedly strong winds blew the defensive shield of chaff away from the target areas - it was decided to incorporate a new ECM fit into a B-52

*The Rockwell B1-B carries a very complex ECM suite which has had a lengthy development period. It is designated to counter all foreseeable threats.*

modification programme known as Rivet Ace, which began in 1974. At first, this involved incorporating updates into the B-52's existing ECM equipment (designated Phase VII update), but at a later date the entire ECM suite was revamped when the B-52 received a new Offensive Avionics System.

This Phase VII ECM equipment included the Westinghouse AN/ALQ-153 tail warning radar, also used in the F-15 and F-111, and the full Northrop AN/ALQ-155 ECM suite, which is based on broad-bandwidth receiving equipment, a signal processor and up to eight transmitters. The system also uses ALT-28 microwave transmitters, mounted in blisters on either side of the B-52's nose under the cockpit, and the ALQ-117 'Pave Mint' defensive jamming system, the equipment for which is mounted in a tail extension. In addition to this electronic jamming equipment, all B-52Gs and Hs can carry up to 192 infra-red countermeasures flares, carried on pylons between the engine installations on each wing.

## UPDATING THE BUFF

The B-52's updated ECM systems were brought into play during the Gulf War, when aircraft were tasked with bombing Iraqi troop positions in and around Kuwait. By the time they were committed to the action, however, the threat posed by Iraqi medium-range SAM systems had been virtually neutralized by Allied strike aircraft, and the B-52s, bombing from high level, were well outside the envelope of other systems such as shoulder-launched SAMs.

The B-52s successor in Strategic Air Command, the Rockwell B-1B, is fitted with a very complex ECM system developed by AIL. Designated ALQ-161, the system is intended to counter air defence, early warning, surveillance and tracking radars, as well as radars associated with interceptors or air-to-air and surface-to-air missiles. In view of the bomber's long projected operational lifetime, much emphasis was given to the use of software-controlled digital equipment capable of being programmed, and in allowing space for additional hardware.

*Apart from its substantial ECM kit, the B-52 has a battery of four 0.5 in guns to defend itself. The bulges above them house the AGS-15 remote fire control radar and an optical sight.*

# PART TWO

# THE AUTOMATED BATTLEFIELD

*The Allied MRLS or Multiple Rocket Launch System was the scourge of the Iraqis during the land battle of Operation Desert Storm.*

# CHAPTER SIX

# THE THIN RED LINE

IN the world of ancient Greece and Rome, it was the heavy infantry - the Greek hoplites, the Macedonian phalangites and the Roman legionaries - who dominated the face of warfare and dictated the rise and fall of empires. Yet if the infantry were to dominate, the battleground had to be carefully chosen.

In AD 9, 'invincible' Rome learned a bitter lesson when three legions were sent on a military expedition against German tribes in the Teutoburger Wald, only to be worn down and systematically destroyed by enemy guerrilla bands, many of which were mounted and were highly mobile.

When the Roman Empire in the west collapsed and the seat of Roman government moved east to Byzantium, it was the Byzantine Army that became the first fully effective force combining all varieties of troops, heavy infantry, light infantry, cavalry and auxiliaries. The former, wearing strong body armour and armed with a lance and either sword or axe, formed a firm base for the rest of the army to pivot upon, standing 16 deep in two lines of battle. Their flanks were protected by the light infantry, wearing only the minimum of body armour to enhance mobility, and armed with bows. Their flanks in turn were guarded by the cavalry, extending the line of battle.

The invention of the firearm did not revolutionize infantry tactics overnight. It took the genius of one man to do that.

He was King Gustavus Adolphus of Sweden, who early in the 17th century formed the Swedish Army's infantry into brigades of two or four regiments, each of which had eight battalions of four companies that were composed of 72 musketeers and 54 pikemen. The infantry were

Not far removed from the time of Napoleon: Italian infantry pose for the camera just before the Battle of Caporetto in 1917.

issued with the first practical cartridges, enabling them to load the charge and bullet in a single operation rather than having to measure out a quantity of powder before each discharge. Firing was by volley of three ranks at a time, the first kneeling, the second stooping and the third standing.

A century later, one of France's finest military commanders, Maurice de Saxe, improved on this structure by creating the army division, a permanent formation incorporating every military unit needed to sustain a campaign. He fully integrated infantry and cavalry tactics, and emphasized the need for intelligent leadership, something he recognized as vital to morale. His ideas were adopted by a man who was to forge the most technically efficient army in Europe, Frederick the Great of Prussia.

Infantry tactics changed little before the end of the 19th century, although they were modified to meet tactical requirements; the British Army, for example, adopted the 'infantry square', a four-sided formation with ranks three deep, as a defence against heavy cavalry. It was used to good effect at Waterloo.

Little serious thought was given to personal protection or camouflage for the infantryman until the British Army began to use khaki in place of the traditional red tunic at the time of the Indian Mutiny. And it was not until 1915 that steel helmets were issued to British troops fighting in France.

The steel helmet remained the infantryman's only form of self-protection until the Second World War, when lorry-borne infantry attached to tank divisions became armoured in their own right with the introduction of armoured personnel carriers.

That war brought other changes too, not least of which was the use of airborne forces to create new fighting zones by dropping large numbers of

In the Second World War, as in the Gulf, the infantry had to do the dirty work. Here GIs ford a river in Germany, April 1945.

men and materials behind enemy lines in comparative secrecy. This concept too was revolutionized by the advent of the helicopter, used by airborne troops on a massive scale in Vietnam and, more recently, in the Gulf War.

Today's infantryman has a formidable technical arsenal at his disposal, in the form of both personal weaponry and backup by air power as well as artillery. The question is not whether he is well equipped to perform his unchanging task, which is to assault and overwhelm the enemy, but whether he can survive the lethal environment of tomorrow's battlefield.

# NO HIDING PLACE The lot of the present-day infantry?

**A**S far as the infantryman is concerned, the war in the Gulf was a one-sided affair. The Iraqi Army of Occupation in Kuwait felt the full weight of the awesome firepower that can be brought to bear on ground forces in modern war; the Coalition forces did not. If war had come on Europe's central front, the picture would have been very different. Infantry on both sides would certainly have suffered appalling casualties.

Such a war would have involved a great deal of fighting in built-up areas, savage close-quarter work where every few yards of ground represent a new, bitterly-contested battleground. This kind of battle is fought with small arms, flame throwers and grenades; in some cases artillery can make a useful contribution, but it is vulnerable to counter-attack.

*A Jaguar fighter-bomber has just released its load to saturate an armoured column with devastating effect. The disadvantage of this form of attack is that the aircraft must overfly its target.*

Tanks are the main support weapon, blasting holes in the walls of buildings for the infantry to pass through, and destroying strong points. Air power plays little part, because of the risk of hitting friendly forces.

### ASSAULT FROM THE AIR

Infantry deployed in the open, perhaps defending a key point, face a different kind of battle. They face bombardment from the air with every conceivable kind of bomb and missile, many of which are capable of penetrating fortified bunkers. Saturation bombing by aircraft such as the B-52, used in both Vietnam and the Gulf War, is a devastating weapon in its own right; a swathe of 50 1,000 lb bombs, even if they fail to hit the target directly, create a blast effect that can kill a person by concussion or cause his stomach to burst.

Infantry caught out in the open may be subjected to another fearsome air-dropped weapon, the Fuel-Air Explosive (FAE). The USAF used this weapon against Iraqi positions in Kuwait, employing a 100 lb

BLU-73B FAE submunition filled with 70 lb of ethylene oxide. Three of these units are released from a 550 lb CBU-55 cluster bomb, their contents being dispersed over the enemy positions to produce an aerosol cloud. This cloud, which becomes very explosive when mixed with air, is detonated when it reaches its optimum size and produces a powerful explosion up to five times as effective, weight for weight, as TNT. When the cloud explodes it produces a fireball that sucks oxygen from the surrounding air, asphyxiating any troops underneath it. Those on the periphery of the explosion suffer fearsome burns.

**WHAT HAPPENS NEXT**
This is only the beginning. Following the air assault comes the artillery bombardment with gun and rocket, and the luckless infantry are now subjected to a lethal rain of fragmentation submunitions which, on exploding, scatter small, jagged chunks of metal over a large area. The fragments are very hot, have razorsharp edges and travel at high speed. Most of the men in range of the fragments are killed, many of them literally shredded.

Those who survive sustain multiple wounds that require immediate treatment by doctors with different medical skills, using specialized scanning

*Ground crew on a desert air base 'somewhere in Saudi Arabia' load cluster-bomb units during Operation Desert Storm.*

equipment only available in the rear areas. Most of the wounded will die.

The bombardment lasts for hours, sometimes days. When it is over the dazed, shocked and bewildered survivors, now barely capable of resistance, are subjected to a full-scale ground assault by armour and enemy infantry. The remaining defensive bunkers are wiped out by missiles originally designed to destroy tanks, by 'smart' mortar munitions and, in the final close-quarter engagement, by phosphorous grenades whose contents burn through human flesh.

Such is the lot of the traditional infantryman in today's high-technology warfare environment - to have the air torn from his lungs, his body ripped to pieces or burned by clinging incendiary devices. But the traditional infantryman may soon be a relic of the past. The leading armies of the world are now turning their attention to a new breed of warrior, men capable of hitting hard and fast while suffering the minimum of casualties. These are the men of the special forces.

# HE WHO DARES WINS

## The secret war where technology comes into its own

**O**N 27 February 1991 - the last day of Operation Desert Storm - Allied Intelligence received some alarming satellite reconnaissance information. It revealed that the Iraqis were moving 26 mobile Scud missile launchers near the country's western border. The indications were that Saddam Hussein was preparing to make a last-ditch barrage attack on Israel.

Since the first Iraqi Scuds hit Israel on 18 January, there had been grave concern among the Allies that the Israelis might retaliate with unconventional weapons. They had issued a warning that they might take such a step by test-firing a nuclear-capable Jericho II missile into the Mediterranean shortly after the first Iraqi attack.

Hunting and destroying the Scud sites, both fixed and mobile, suddenly assumed paramount importance, and a high proportion of the Allied air commitment was diverted to this task.

The biggest problem was locating the mobile Scud launchers, which moved rapidly from place to place once they had fired their missiles. This high-priority task was assigned to Allied special forces troops, American commandos - the famous 'Green Berets' and a highly secret US unit called Delta Force - and the British Special Air Service.

### BRITS, YANKS AND LASERS

Although the special forces got up to some extraordinary things in the Gulf War, such as kidnapping Iraqi officers, cutting communications deep inside Iraq, and on one occasion even stealing a SAM missile in a daring operation using helicopters in Iraqi markings, their primary role was target designation, illuminating targets for strike aircraft equipped with laser-guided weapons. This technique was also applied with considerable success to 'Scud hunting'.

In action against the Scud launchers in western Iraq - the ones threatening Israel - Britain's SAS operated with Delta Force in a special 'fusion cell' under Major General Wayne Downing, commander of the Pentagon's counter-terrorist units. The SAS and Delta Force were old colleagues, having co-operated in anti-terrorist work many times in the past.

The SAS teams were airlifted into Iraq by RAF Chinook helicopters of No 7 (Special Duties) Squadron, which were fitted with multi-barrel 7.62

mm guns capable of firing 6,000 rounds per minute, satellite communications equipment, 'Have Quick' secure speech radio equipment and infra-red jammers.

The Chinooks also carried the SAS men's favourite transport: either a modified open-topped Land Rover called the 'Pink Panther', or a 'Dune Buggy', specially designed for fast movement over desert terrain. Both had a three-man crew and carried two grenade launchers, a 7.62 mm machine gun (firing forwards)

*These Chinook helicopters of No 7 Squadron are rarely seen and now sport 'experimental night camouflage' as worn in the Gulf.*

and a 12.7 mm Browning on a rear swivel mount.

The vehicles were also equipped with satellite navigation and communications system. Delta Force used similar 'Dune Buggies' and equipment. They were airlifted by CH-53 'Pave Low' helicopters, as were Green Beret units operating elsewhere.

In a series of lightning night raids, the British and

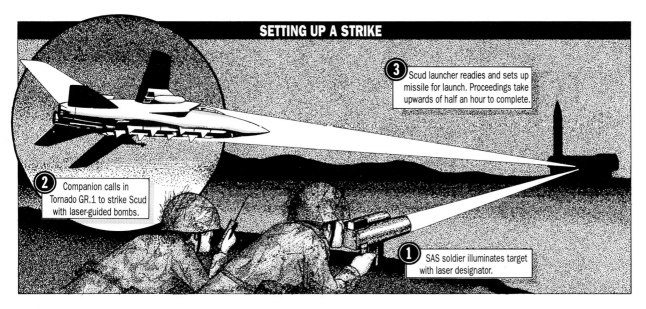

## SETTING UP A STRIKE

**3** Scud launcher readies and sets up missile for launch. Proceedings take upwards of half an hour to complete.

**2** Companion calls in Tornado GR.1 to strike Scud with laser-guided bombs.

**1** SAS soldier illuminates target with laser designator.

American commandos began systematically destroying the command and control centres that supplied the Scud sites with their target information, and also struck hard at storage depots supplying rocket fuel and other facilities.

When a launcher was located, they flashed its co-ordinates via satellite to base and called in an air strike, designating the target with their laser equipment, holding the beam steady on the target while the bomb rode down the laser to strike home.

In two weeks, they were responsible for the destruction of at least 12 Iraqi missiles and their associated equipment.

The high point came on 27 February, when Delta Force and the SAS, supported by A-10 Thunderbolt IIs, were hurled against the 26 mobile Scuds about to be launched against Israel. They destroyed all 26.

The 'Scud hunt' had been a classic special forces operation, its success the end product of many years of specialist training.

It cost the US commandos 11 men missing, presumed killed in action, the SAS one man dead and seven captured in fierce battles with Iraqi troops. It kept Israel out of the war.

# SMALLER, LIGHTER BUT STILL LETHAL
## The saga of the shrinking weapon

THE arsenal of personal weapons that high technology will be capable of providing over the next twenty years or so is likely to change the infantryman's image and effectiveness out of all recognition.

Infantry weapons are undergoing constant changes; the arms themselves are becoming smaller and lighter, as are the bullets they fire. The killing power of a bullet is determined by its mass and the speed at which it hits the target: if new propellants can increase its speed, the round can be made lighter while still inflicting the same degree of damage as a heavier one of an earlier era.

As rounds reduce in size, so does the gun itself; compared with a Lewis Gun or Lee Enfield rifle of the Great War, the modern-day SA-80 rifle is half the size of its earlier counterpart.

### NEW ROUNDS FOR A NEW ERA
Such hypervelocity bullets are already in use with the German Heckler and Koch G11 Advanced Combat Rifle (ACR), which carries 50 rounds in a magazine mounted above the barrel. The G11's outer casing is constructed mainly of carbon reinforced plastic, which seals in the firing mechanism and other inner working parts to protect them from dirt; it also makes the weapon easier to decontaminate in a nuclear-chemical-biological environment.

Another advanced combat rifle is the American 5.56/4.32 mm weapon, while the British Army uses the SA80. All these advanced rifles are fitted with optical sights. Future rifles will most likely combine the best attributes of these modern designs, and may also incorporate thermal or radar imaging sights as well.

The next stage in the development of the personal infantry weapon will be the so-called rail gun, an electromagnetic weapon that uses kinetic energy to boost the velocity of a round. It generates electromagnetic energy in twin metallic rails running parallel to the gun barrel, or in a coil wrapped around it. A bullet made of plastic or some other non-conducting material is injected between the rails, and a circuit between them is completed by conductors at the base of the bullet. The round is then speeded up by the resulting massive current. This acceleration is generated by a phenomenon known as the 'Lorenz' effect, which is created by the movement of a current across a magnetic field.

Experimental rail guns have already fired rounds at 32,800 ft/sec. In comparison, the speed of an average rifle bullet is 2,600 ft/sec. In its present development stage, however, the rail gun is a large, cumbersome piece of apparatus, which needs an external power source. Much work remains to be done on it before it can be refined to the status of an infantry weapon.

### MERLIN AND MILAN
Mortars have also been revolutionized with the introduction of 'smart' mortar munitions like the British Aerospace Dynamics Merlin, which is designed to be fired from standard 81 mm and 82 mm mortars to give infantry and marine forces a highly effective capability against tanks and other armoured vehicles.

Merlin is launched in the same way as a

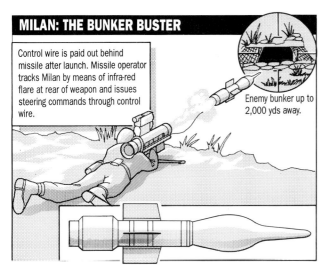

## MILAN: THE BUNKER BUSTER

Control wire is paid out behind missile after launch. Missile operator tracks Milan by means of infra-red flare at rear of weapon and issues steering commands through control wire.

Enemy bunker up to 2,000 yds away.

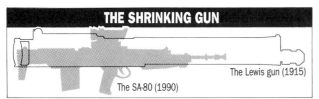

## THE SHRINKING GUN

The Lewis gun (1915)

The SA-80 (1990)

conventional mortar bomb, from an upward pointing barrel. After launch, six rear-mounted fins are deployed to provide aerodynamic stability, followed by four forward-mounted, or canard, fins to provide directional control. The bomb's millimetric seeker is activated as Merlin approaches the top of its trajectory and searches first for moving, then stationary, targets. Having acquired a target, the seeker provides the necessary information to the bomb's guidance system to ensure impact with the most vulnerable areas on top of the armoured vehicle.

As far as defensive infantry weapons are concerned, the most important development has been the man-portable surface-to-air missile. These weapons are now in widespread use throughout the world. This has caused severe problems for low-level strike aircraft, which are now very vulnerable to attack from an area that was not originally envisaged when the aircraft was designed.

Sometimes, infantry weapons prove highly adaptable to a role for which they were never intended. An example is MILAN (*Missile d'Infanterie Légère Anti-Char*) a French-designed surface-to-surface weapon originally intended for anti-tank use. During the Falklands War, it was found that when MILAN's 3.19 lb warhead hit a hillside dugout, its crushing impact was reinforced by a shock wave and sheet of flame that almost invariably killed everyone inside. MlLAN's computer-controlled, wire-guided system gives it a 98 per cent chance of a direct hit at ranges between 230 and 2,000 yards. The missile weighs 24 lb, while the launching base and guidance unit weigh only 36 lb. It is fired over the-shoulder by one man operating as part of a team of three.

In the next century, armaments like Merlin and MILAN may be joined by offensive laser weapons designed to blind the pilots of incoming aircraft. These laser dazzle sights (LDS) are already in operational use and are deployed on board Royal Navy warships. They were said to have been used during the 1982 Falklands War, although this has been denied by the UK Ministry of Defence.

*A British infantryman peers through the sight of his SA-80 assault rifle. Its mechanism is completely sealed in for protection from dirt.*

# THE ULTIMATE WARRIORS Tin soldiers of the 21st century

**R**OBOT devices have been around for a long time on the battlefield. During the Second World War, for example, the Germans used a remotely-controlled miniature tank called Goliath, packed with explosives, to blast holes in enemy defences, and modern warfare sees the widespread use of remotely-controlled unmanned aircraft.

Turning the infantryman into a robot presents a much more formidable challenge and yet the first tentative steps have already been taken towards just that goal. As long ago as 1983, the American firm Odetics Inc., of Anaheim, California, produced the world's first mobile, multifunction walking machine. Named Odex I, the device is the prototype of a new generation of robot machines - called functionoids - which may begin to replace human beings in a variety of tasks in the 21st century.

Odex I is a six-legged robot that can walk over uneven ground, climb and descend while carrying a stable platform and lift objects many times its own weight. It has a so-called 'tripod gait', supporting itself on three of its articulated legs while using the other three to move forward. This motion is continuous, so that the three legs on the ground only have to support the machine momentarily. The robot has a forward speed of about three miles per hour, equalling a human's brisk walking pace.

Odex I weighs 374 lb and is capable of lifting up to 2,000 lb with all six legs on the ground. It can also lift 1,800 lb while walking slowly, and about 1,000 lb at its normal walking speed. Powered by a self-contained 24-volt battery, it can operate for one hour without recharging.

The device is controlled via a radio link, with its operator using a joystick-type control to issue commands to its computer. Odex I can assume several different profiles, rising to a maximum height of over six feet to look over obstacles and compressing itself to only three feet to creep under obstacles.

### THE ROBOT IS DEAD, LONG LIVE THE ROBOT
Functionoids now under development for military purposes, in the United States and elsewhere, are equipped with stereo TV systems with ultrasonic equipment to provide depth perception by measuring dimensions and distances within the robot's line of sight. Tactile sensors for robotic limbs are also under development; these will give the robot a sense of touch which, if not as sensitive as a human being's, will provide it with the necessary capability to perform delicate tasks without being directly controlled by a human source.

The US and Soviet armies both have a serious requirement for military functionoids to carry out relatively simple tasks, such as reconnaissance and surveillance, mine clearance, transporting supplies and ammunition. Scientists are optimistic that they can create a 'thinking' robot, capable of carrying out such tasks autonomously, with only very general human instructions, by the end of this century.

Curiously enough, the study of robotics as a military science runs closely parallel to the development of robot devices for use in the much more mundane environment of farming. At the French Institute for Agricultural Engineering

*This is how a warrior of the 21st century might look. He is completely protected by body armour and carries a variety of weapons.*

## THE 21ST CENTURY SOLDIER

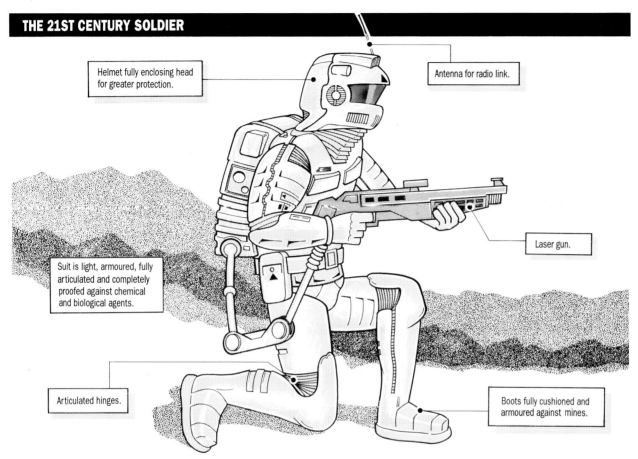

Helmet fully enclosing head for greater protection.

Antenna for radio link.

Laser gun.

Suit is light, armoured, fully articulated and completely proofed against chemical and biological agents.

Articulated hinges.

Boots fully cushioned and armoured against mines.

Research in Montpellier, for instance, scientists are trying to develop a robot fruit picker which will have an element of human sense. It will be capable of identifying ripe fruit, even behind leaves, and pick it with the speed of a good manual worker.

Such robots are essentially computer-controlled limbs. They have the ability to move, to manipulate and to touch with the aid of sensors, to see with television eyes, and to taste with chemical sensors. Robotic speech, too, is constantly being refined using the latest electronic techniques.

The robot is, therefore, much more than a mechanical humanoid. It has its own memory, its own capacity to learn, and - if its maker so desires - it can be endowed with a capability to defend itself. High-technology weapons such as the Cruise missiles are lethal robots, programmed to make their own decisions about which flight path to follow and, if needs be, to make mid-flight corrections in order to attack alternative targets. Scientific space vehicles, which are exploratory robots, are also capable of making their own decisions to some degree, should commands from Earth fail to reach them.

But it is on the farm and in the factory that some of the biggest advances in robotics are now being made, in the context of machines that can duplicate human dexterity and intelligence.

Military scientists are keeping a close watch on proceedings in the hope that their agricultural colleagues will achieve a breakthrough.

### THE TIN SOLDIER?

Even if this breakthrough is made by the turn of the century, there will be an enormous gap between the operational use of such robots and the creation of a 'tin soldier' with an ability to fight and make instant tactical decisions.

At the moment, only the human brain can do that. The practical application of cybernetics - the study of communication and control mechanisms in living beings and machines, the ultimate goal of which is the creation of a robot brain able to perform all the functions of its human counterpart - is certain to make enormous strides over the next couple of decades, but the creation of an automatic fighting man is only a dream for the time being.

# CHAPTER SEVEN

# TANKS - THE MODERN CAVALRY

IT *was a British engineer, Lieutenant-Colonel Ernest Swinton, who in September 1914 recognized that the war in Europe was likely to become bogged down in a stalemate of trench warfare, and proposed the building of armoured fighting machines capable of breaking through enemy trench systems.*

*The French had similar proposals, although at first their idea involved only armoured tractors designed to break through barbed wire entanglements.*

*The first attack by British Mk I tanks took place on 15 September 1916 and met with only limited success. On 20 November 1917, the British launched the first tank offensive in history, when 476 tanks forced a 12-mile breach in the strongest sector of the Hindenburg Line at Cambrai. Whereas the Germans remained*

American tanks of the 326th Btn, 311 Tank Center, move forward into action in the autumn of 1918, near the River Meuse, France.

*deficient in armour - they never produced more than 13 tanks in any one battle - the British had a total of 1,184 tanks on the Western Front by July 1918. The first ever tank-v-tank engagement took place on 24 April 1918, when three British Mk IVs engaged three German heavy A7Vs. One of the latter was knocked out, although not before the Germans had disabled three lightly armoured Whippet tanks that had been shooting up infantry.*

*On many occasions the British tanks, because of their ability to react quickly to a situation, were able to disrupt German infantry attacks in open country. Often, the movement of the armour was directed by army co-operation aircraft. The biggest tank action of the war took place on 8 August 1918, when an advance by 604 Allied tanks took an exhausted German army corps completely by surprise and overran it.*

*The lessons of the First World War were not lost on Germany's military leaders under the Nazi regime. Although the British were the first to experiment with a fully mechanized fighting*

A German crew pose in front of their Tiger during the Soviet campaign of 1942.

force in the 1920s, they tended to use their armour for direct infantry support or for reconnaissance. The Germans adopted a different philosophy. Under the guidance of General Hans von Seeckt, they developed the tank as an instrument of mobile warfare and formulated the classic Blitzkrieg (Lightning War) tactics in which their Panzer divisions, preceded by ground attack aircraft like the Junkers Ju 87 Stuka dive-bomber, plunged deep into enemy territory and created corridors that were then exploited by mechanized infantry.

Such tactics worked well in the Battle of France and in Africa's Western Desert, although in the latter case the Germans were foiled by Allied air supremacy. They also worked well in the early phase of the attack on Russia, but received a shock in the form of Russia's heavily-armoured KV-l and T-34 tanks, whose 76 mm guns could penetrate the Wehrmacht tanks' armour while remaining immune to German ammunition.

To meet this new challenge, the Germans launched a crash industrial programme to build a new generation of massive, heavily armoured fighting vehicles. Two of its products were the Tiger and the Panther. The 43-ton Panther tank, with frontal armour of 83 mm thickness, a speed of 28 mph and a main armament of one 75 mm gun was, undoubtedly, the best tank produced by any side during the Second World War, and elements of its design were reflected in post-war AFVs like the British Centurion.

The 49-ton Centurion Mk 3 of the late 1950s, with an electronically-stabilized 83.4 mm, and later 105 mm gun, was an outstanding example. When it began to be phased out of British service in 1960, other nations were keen to acquire it. So good a design was the Centurion that today it is still in service with many nations. Together with the American M48, it wrought havoc on Egypt's Russian-built tanks in the 1967 Arab-Israeli War.

These two machines were the progenitors of a line of armoured fighting vehicles which culminated in two excellent designs that saw action in the Gulf. Capable of taking on the best Soviet-designed equipment and destroying it with almost ridiculous ease, America's M1 Abrams and Britain's Challenger will certainly rank alongside the Panther as the most effective tanks ever built.

# AMERICA'S NO 1 TANK The Guard destroyer

EVERY war produces its quota of classic remarks by military commanders. The Gulf War was no exception.

On Tuesday, 26 February 1991, day three of the 100-hour war against the Iraqi forces in Kuwait, tanks of the US 1st Armored Division encountered units of the allegedly élite Iraqi Republican Guard. The Divisional Commander, Major-General Ronald Griffiths, radioed his deputy, who was riding with the armoured spearhead. '*Understand we are engaging the Medina Division?*' he said.

'*Negative, sir,*' came the reply. '*We are destroying the Medina Division.*'

The destruction was carried out by a combination of close support air power and the 1st Armored Division's M1A1 Abrams main battle tanks (MBTs). Like the British Challenger, they were seeing combat for the first time; also like Challenger, their prowess against the Republican Guard's Russian-built T-72s exceeded anyone's expectations.

## A LONG, INVOLVED PRODUCTION HISTORY

The M1 Abrams is the end product of a long and stormy period of tank development during which the US Army sought a replacement for its M60 series of main battle tanks, which were standard equipment throughout the 1960s and 1970s. Two prototypes of the new tank were built, designated XM1. On the US Army's insistence they were fitted with British-developed Chobham armour and mounted an M68 105 mm rifled cannon, a gun with increased range and firepower that enabled it to keep pace with the latest developments in Soviet armour. The MBT's secondary armament consisted of one 50 calibre and two 7.62 mm machine guns.

One XM1 was built by Chrysler and the other by General Motors. One was powered by a diesel engine, the other by a 1,500 hp Avco Lycoming AGT-1500 gas turbine. Trials began in 1976, and it was the turbine-powered Chrysler vehicle that was selected for production under the designation M1. The first production M1 was handed over to the US Army on 28 February 1980.

The gas turbine engine, although hungry for fuel, gives the Abrams an excellent performance and, unlike diesel-engined vehicles, has the advantage of being exceptionally quiet, emitting only a muted whine even at full power. It gives the 60-ton tank a road speed of 44 mph and a cross-country speed of 35 mph. An engine change takes only an hour, compared with four hours for the diesel engine in the M60.

The production M1A1 Abrams saw the 105 mm gun replaced by the harder-hitting M256 120 mm smooth-bore cannon, a German-designed weapon. The tank's fire control system comprises a fully integrated laser rangefinder and digital computer; the latter processes information on wind, temperature, ammunition type, vehicle movement and equipment sensors, giving the Abrams a 90 per cent first round hit probability even when shooting at speed.

An infra-red thermal imaging system allows the commander and gunner to engage targets by day, night, in haze, in fog or in the smoke of battle.

## THE NEW, IMPROVED MODEL

The Abrams is undergoing a number of improvements which will make it a viable fighting vehicle for years to come. These include an independent thermal imaging system for the tank commander, enabling him to track and identify targets while the gunner is engaging a separate one; a computerized Battlefield Management System (BMS) designed to take much of the tactical workload from the commander; an identification friend/foe system; new laser rangefinders with built-

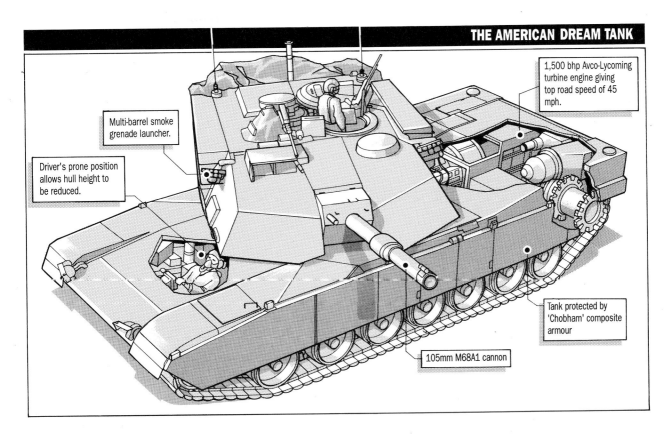

**THE AMERICAN DREAM TANK**

Multi-barrel smoke grenade launcher.

Driver's prone position allows hull height to be reduced.

1,500 bhp Avco-Lycoming turbine engine giving top road speed of 45 mph.

Tank protected by 'Chobham' composite armour

105mm M68A1 cannon

in safeguards against vision damage; and added hull protection with an armour mesh made of depleted uranium. This is two and a half times as dense as similar mesh made of steel, and provides greater protection against the latest shaped-charge anti-tank missile warheads.

Left and below: *During combat in the Gulf War the Abrams main battle tank proved itself as a tough and hard-hitting fighting vehicle capable of destroying the Russian-built Iraqi Republican armour with ease. On the German Plain it would perform to the same high and efficient standard.*

# RISING TO THE CHALLENGE  The world's most advanced tank?

ON Monday 25 February 1991, 157 Challenger 1 main battle tanks, and 135 Warrior armoured personnel carriers of the British Army's 4th and 7th Armoured Brigades, punched their way into Kuwait through a series of gaps that had been blasted through the Iraqi defences by combat engineers of the American 1st Infantry Division.

The Challengers - their task to protect the flank of the US VII Corps and to destroy the Iraqi armoured reserve inside Kuwait - plunged on at speed. At 11 pm they made contact with the enemy, overrunning a battalion headquarters and capturing its commander. During the night they sliced through the Iraqi 12th Armoured Division and then swung east to engage the enemy's 6th Armoured Division. The following day saw them astride the Kuwait City-Basra highway, having destroyed at least 300 enemy tanks for no loss to themselves through enemy fire. One British tankman compared the operation to a video game in which they 'gobbled up Iraqi divisions like Pac-man.'

## AFTER CENTURION AND CHIEFTAIN

Britain's Challenger 1 was developed by Vickers Defence Systems from their earlier Chieftain, which succeeded the well-tried Centurion in the mid-1960s. It seemed that the Chieftain would assure Britain's lead in tank development. It set a new standard for main battle tanks with its extremely well-designed armour and powerful 120 mm gun. But in one respect the Chieftain was too far ahead of its time.

It used a multi-fuel engine, a piece of advanced technology that created many development problems. These were eventually overcome and, as time went by, the Chieftain was fitted with a much improved equipment, including a laser-directed fire control system.

The Chieftain was bought by Iran under the Shah's regime, and later proved itself beyond all doubt in the war against Iraq. The Iranians ordered an improved version, the *Shir*, from Vickers Defence Systems, but this deal fell through when the Shah was deposed. The British Army accelerated its programme to purchase a new main battle tank, and the partly-built tanks for Iran, with modifications, were developed into the Challenger 1.

The new tank was a promising design. It featured many refinements, such as Chobham composite armour - laminated protective plates that absorb the energy of an anti-tank shell or missile, and a

**BRITAINS LATEST WINNING FORMULA**

Commanders and gunners laser range finder and sight.

Thermal imaging equipment

Smoke canister and grenade dispenser

Driver night vision capable periscope

'Chobham' protective armour

*A view of the exterior turret of the new Challenger 2 MBT. It has now been ordered by the British Government to replace Challenger 1.*

serviceability rate, higher than that of the Abrams.

The performance of Challenger 1 in Desert Storm, 'the most effective armoured performance that this country has ever produced,' to quote British Defence Secretary Tom King, underlined Vickers' valid claim that Challenger 2 was operationally the best tank for the British Army.

The use of the best proven technology available makes Challenger 2 the world's most formidable fighting vehicle. Its fire control system is fully computerized, and its improved 120 mm rifled tank gun uses new ammunition designed to overcome all threats in the foreseeable future. Like its predecessor, it is heavily protected by Chobham armour, and its turret can withstand the impact of all existing tank-fired ammunition. Adding to the safety factors, all explosive ammunition is stored under armour and below the turret ring.

Challenger 2 is also a 'stealth' tank; its hull and turret have built-in technology that make the vehicle more difficult to detect by enemy radar. Moreover, many of its components are interchangeable with those of Challenger 1, alongside which it will operate, simplifying the ever-present spare parts problem.

revolutionary night fighting system, using thermal imaging that displayed the target on a TV screen. The tank commander or gunner simply had to sight on the target, push a ranging button to activate the electronic devices, and squeeze the trigger to score a first-round hit with the 120 mm gun at a range of up to 3,300 yards.

## A DEBATE ON PERFORMANCE

There were ongoing doubts about Challenger 1's ability to perform well in battle. It was compared unfavourably in some military circles with the American Abrams and the German Leopard, particularly during manoeuvres and gunnery exercises with NATO in Germany. Such doubts were reflected in the reluctance of the UK Ministry of Defence to make a final decision on the procurement of Challenger 2, the next-generation main battle tank.

It took a war to dispel the doubts. In the Iraqi desert, apart from their excellent combat performance, the Challenger 1s of the British 1st Armoured Division achieved a 95 per cent

*Scourge of Iraq's armour: a Challenger 1 main battle tank churns up the unusually damp sand in the Saudi desert.*

# IMPROVED WARHEADS V IMPROVED ARMOUR
## Bang, flash and squash!

**O**PERATION Desert Storm saw the use of virtually the whole arsenal of Allied anti-tank weaponry. The Iraqis had Soviet-supplied anti-tank missiles too, but they were designed to be air-launched by helicopters - and the latter were unable to operate because of total Allied air supremacy. This was one of the factors that made the armoured battle such a one-sided affair.

### SAGGER, SPIGOT, SPANDREL AND SPIRAL

Iraq's arsenal included the AT-2 Swatter, a Soviet wire-guided anti-tank missile. In service since the 1960s, it is carried by the Mi-24 Hind helicopter and can also be mounted on the Soviet BRDM amphibious vehicle; it powered by a solid propellant rocket motor and its warhead can penetrate 19 in of armour plate. Its maximum range is 2,700 yards. Swatter was the first of a family of Soviet anti-tank weapons that includes the AT-3 Sagger, AT-4 Spigot, AT-5 Spandrel and AT-6 Spiral. The latter carries a 22 lb warhead and has a range of five miles. It is standard equipment on the Mi-24 and Mi-28.

The principal types of anti-armour missile in service with the US Army are the FGM-77A Dragon, AGM-114 Hellfire and TOW. The Dragon, known as

the M-47 in the US Army, is produced by McDonnell Douglas/Raytheon and carries a five-and-a-quarter-pound hollow charge warhead that can penetrate 20 in of armour at a maximum range of 1,200 yards. Hellfire, developed by Rockwell and Martin Marietta, is a devastating anti-tank weapon carried by US Army AH-64 Apache and US Marines AH-1W SuperCobra helicopters. In the Gulf War it was used against bunkers and radar installations, as well as against enemy armour. Hellfire carries a 5 lb warhead and has a five-mile range.

### THE TOW FAMILY

The Hughes BGM-71 TOW-1 missile is in widespread use throughout NATO, including the British Army, where it is fitted to Army Air Corps Lynx helicopters. It entered service in 1981 and was followed by the improved TOW-2 and TOW-2A. The latter has a secondary charge in its nose probe. Intended to pre-detonate the reactive armour of Soviet tanks, this allows the main charge to penetrate the tank's exposed main armour. TOW-2 carries a 13 lb warhead and has a maximum range of 4,100 yards.

The Euromissile consortium produces two in-service anti-tank systems, HOT and MILAN. HOT, a heavy long-range weapon, is in service with 15 countries and can be ground- or air-launched. Its hollow-charge warhead contains over 6 lb of explosive and can penetrate 32 in of armour when impacting head-on, or eight in of armour at an angle of 65°. HOT 2 has a heavier warhead of increased diameter, containing 9 lb of explosive. Its maximum range is 4,400 yards, The other missile, MILAN, has a computer-controlled, wire-guidance fire control system that gives it a 98 per cent chance of scoring a direct hit at ranges between 230 and 2,000 yards. Its three-and-a-quarter-pound warhead can penetrate 15 in of armour at an angle of 65°. MILAN has proved devastating against fortified bunkers and trenches.

### VERSATILE SWINGFIRE

One of the world's most effective anti-tank missiles is the British Aerospace Swingfire. It can be launched

*The BAe Swingfire anti-tank missile being launched from an FV102 combat vehicle.*

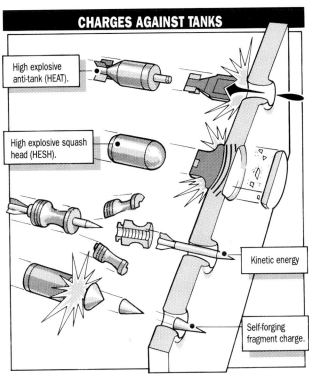

**CHARGES AGAINST TANKS**

High explosive anti-tank (HEAT).

High explosive squash head (HESH).

Kinetic energy

Self-forging fragment charge.

from an FV102 Striker combat vehicle, which carries five missiles, or from a four-launcher pallet controlled by an infantry team. Swingfire has a thermal imaging sighting system which detects a target by sensing the radiation emitted by the tank in contrast to the background. The missile has a 15 lb hollow-charge warhead and a maximum range of 4,400 yards.

## LASERS ENTER THE FRAY

Missile systems such as TOW, HOT and Swingfire will be replaced in the late 1990s by a new system called TRIGAT, jointly developed by Britain, France and Germany. It will come in two versions, one with a laser guidance and the other with a passive infra-red system to give it a fire-and-forget capability. The two versions will have respective ranges of 1 and a quarter and 2 and a half miles.

Another useful anti-tank weapon is the British Ajax system. This consists of a rocket launcher which can be concealed near likely enemy tank-routes and fires automatically when its sensors detect possible tanks.

*Top: HOT is an air-launched, anti-tank weapon, whilst Ajax (right), is an expendable one-shot missile which is remotely controlled.*

# CHAPTER EIGHT

# MINES - THE UNSEEN KILLERS

IT *was the operational use of the tank during the latter stages of the First World War that led to the development of the land mine, in an effort to counter this new form of mechanized warfare.*

*Early mines consisted of heavy charges of high explosive buried in the ground and fitted with detonators that exploded under the pressure of a heavy weight. In one attack on the Hindenburg Line on 29 September 1918, ten American tanks were destroyed when they passed through an old and forgotten anti-tank minefield.*

The biggest bang ever. During the First World War the Allies exploded a mine that is still regarded as being the largest of its kind ever detonated.

*The development of anti-personnel mines was a natural progression, and formed an important part of the arsenals of most armies at the outbreak of the Second World War.*

*The conventional metallic anti-tank and anti-personnel mines remained in use until the end of the war. By then, the Germans in particular had added many more efficient mines to their arsenal which were hard to locate and neutralize. Wooden, glass and bakelite bodies thwarted electronic detectors, and ingenious booby-trap devices were added to make manual mine clearance a very hazardous job. The British put a great deal of thought into mine clearance, producing devices such as the 'flail' tank which played a vital part in clearing paths through minefields on the Normandy beaches.*

A lance corporal in the Royal Engineer's Bomb Disposal squad inspects a recently planted enemy mine.

Soviet mines came in all shapes and sizes. The Russians made the most use of mine warfare as a tactic during the Second World War.

*Russian land mines caused severe problems for the invading German Armies. The Russians made wider use of mines than any other belligerent. During the crucial battle for the Kursk salient in the summer of 1943, the Soviets laid 1,500 anti-tank and 1,700 anti-personnel mines along every half-mile of the front. Most of these had to be cleared by hand. The Russian method of clearing enemy minefields quickly was very simple; troops serving in penal battalions were compelled to charge over them. The Iranians used similar tactics in their war with Iraq.*

*Today, laying mines by hand is still the most effective way of concealing them, although the process is time-consuming. So is lifting them. In the aftermath of the Falklands War, Royal Engineers and other British troops had to contend with more than 12,000 Argentinian mines, grouped in 185 separate minefields in the Port Stanley area. Many of them had been scattered indiscriminately; Argentine infantry,*

*marines and some artillery units had been issued with mines during the later stages of the war, and had laid them without keeping records of their whereabouts.*

*To make matters worse, the British troops' available mine detectors were virtually useless when it came to locating the modern, sophisticated Argentine, Italian and Spanish mines that had been used, many of them made of plastic. Detection had to be carried out by means of a mine prodder, rather like a long meat skewer with a handle on, or by poking the ground with a bayonet. It was dangerous work, and resulted in serious injury to some of the troops involved.*

*During the Gulf War, mines were widely scattered by Allied aircraft over Iraqi roads and sites that were likely to be used by mobile Scud launchers, while area denial mines were scattered by Tornado strike aircraft during their low-level attacks on enemy airfields. Modern mine-laying systems are capable of laying 600 mines per hour with accuracy.*

# THE JUMPING MINE And other intelligent killers

**G**ERMANY was at the forefront of mine warfare technology during the Second World War. The same is true today, for some of the world's most astonishing 'smart' mines have been developed by the German defence company, Messerschmitt-Bolkow-Blohm (MBB). One of the latest is a mine that moves around the battlefield in a random and unpredictable manner; MBB calls it a 'stochastic' mine.

A series of small explosive charges, programmed to explode in a random sequence, makes the mine bounce along the ground for up to 1,200 yards. When the mine comes into contact with a large metallic object such as an armoured vehicle, the latter's magnetic field activates the mine's explosive charge, which can be up to 33 lb in weight - enough to inflict considerable damage on even a main battle tank. Some of the latest stochastic mines can bounce around the battlefield for up to three days.

A further variant is a jumping mine; this can be triggered to jump into an area that has just been cleared of other mines, taking advancing armour by surprise.

Above and opposite: *Clearing mines during an army exercise. Mines presented enormous problems in the Gulf as they would have on NATO's central front.*

## MINE-HEADS WITH MINI-COMPUTERS

Some mines have built-in micro-processors, which can be programmed so that no two mines behave in

**THE CHOPPER STOPPER**

As the helicopter prepares to land in a defended area, the downwash from its rotor blades activates the mine's detonator. This can be a very simple mechanism in the form of a small windmill device which turns in response to the downward air pressure and compresses the detonator cap, or a more sensitive device which senses when the helicopter is within lethal damage range.

exactly the same way. The mines use their 'intelligence' to determine the bearing of an oncoming target and fire sub-munitions at it from a distance. The British Army already has a mine that can fire sub-munitions at tanks from up to 500 ft away. Developed by British Aerospace and called an 'off-route' mine, this weapon can be concealed close to routes likely to be used by enemy armour. Its sensors can detect a moving tank and distinguish it from less important vehicles; they can also differentiate between advancing enemy tanks and friendly armour moving in the opposite direction. Some of the latest 'listening' mines have sensitive microphones linked to a computer system that can not only distinguish between tanks and other fighting vehicles, but also analyse the tank's acoustic 'signature' to determine whether it is, say, a T-72 tank or a T-80.

## MINES THAT HAVE TWO MINDS

Most intelligent mines have a dual sensory system comprising a microphone and an optical sensor. When the microphone detects an approaching tank, the mine extends its optical eye on the end of a thin

periscope. The eye, which is either an infra-red sensor or a radar beam, scans the area for something that looks like a tank. It also directs a laser beam on to the approaching target to gather distance and bear-ing information, so that the microprocessor can pass precise details of the location to the mine. Then it waits until the object is within range before firing its ammunition.

One major advance in recent years has been the development of 'communicating minefields'. As the name suggests this consists of a network of intel-ligent mines. These mines can tell when a tank has entered the minefield, count how many tanks have entered in a given time, and pass on this information by radio or optical fibres to other mines in the network. The whole minefield operates as a single entity; it can wait until a number of targets have entered the area and then activate the mines nearest to the enemy armour.

In the 1960s, the Vietcong, using their con-siderable powers of innovation, modified Russian-built land mines as weapons against American helicopters by attaching a simple windmill device to the mine's detonating mechanism. When a helicopter hovered overhead, the downwash from its blades turned the windmill, and this detonated the weapon. Similar mines were used by the Iraqis during the Gulf War.

# BREACHING THE BARRIER Snakes, ploughs and rollers

**T**ODAY'S combat engineers have a considerable array of mine clearance systems at their disposal. One of the most basic systems is still the flail tank, developed by the British during the Second World War for the assault on the Normandy beaches. This consists of a rotating drum with chains suspended from it, attached to the front of an armoured vehicle. As the drum rotates, the chains strike the ground and detonate any mines that are activated by pressure or vibration. As the width of the flail drum exceeds the width of the armoured vehicle, the latter clears a broad swathe through the minefield, opening a path for other tanks.

An added advantage is that several tanks clearing paths through a minefield create a considerable amount of dust and smoke from exploding mines, obscuring the advance of friendly armour.

## ROLLERS AND PLOUGHS

One variant of the flail tank is the Mine Roller. These machines work on the same principle as the flail. Attached to the front of a tank, they exert sufficient downward pressure on the ground to detonate mines, but are too heavy and solid themselves to be affected by the explosions.

The mine plough is the most effective combat-proven solution to the anti-tank mine problem, and has several significant advantages over all the other systems. It physically removes mines from the path of an armoured vehicle, reducing any doubts about whether a mine has been neutralized or not. It can also be carried by all heavy armoured vehicles without significantly reducing their mobility. An additional asset is that it can be brought into use instantly, whenever a minefield threat is recognized.

One of the world's leading exponents of mine plough technology is the British company, Pearson Engineering, based at Newcastle upon Tyne in northern England.

The company's products have evolved over the past decade to meet the growing problem presented by scatterable or remotely delivered mines, which can rapidly be sown in the path of any mobile unit. Pearson's approach has been to develop a range of bulldozing and mine clearing equipment that is interchangeable between combat vehicles without inhibiting their primary role. Self-contained power packs and a common mounting system mean that any tank, with the appropriate mounting points fitted, can be very rapidly converted into a powerful

*An American M-48 tank travelling at speed, using its combat dozer blade.*

earthmover or minefield breaching vehicle.

Careful design of the equipment means that any tank converted in this way does not lose its combat effectiveness as a fighting vehicle. The combined anchor/dozer blade of the Challenger Armoured Repair and Recovery Vehicle (ARRV), provides a good example, combining high efficiency in both roles with minimum weight and maximum vehicle mobility.

The Pathfinder marker system displays similar flexibility.

Intended to sign the boundaries of dangerous areas with marker rods, this device fires reusable rods into the ground using compressed air, which makes for low inservice costs. It is easily fitted and is rapidly interchangeable between say, a main battle tank fitted with a mine plough and an armoured personnel carrier, marking a contaminated area or approach lanes to a minefield.

## SNAKES THAT SAVE LIVES

One very effective method of clearing a path through the minefield is to use an explosive hose system such as the British Army's 'Giant Viper'. The advantage of such systems is that they can be fired into minefields across anti-tank ditches or defensive ramparts (berms), and can also be used to destroy barbed wire fortifications.

The Giant Viper system comprises a flexible rocket-launched hose, up to 600 ft long and packed with explosives, mounted on a trailer towed behind an armoured vehicle. When the hose lands its explosive charge detonates, setting off any pressure or contact mines beneath it and for some distance on either side.

All these vehicles and appliances were to be put to the test in the Gulf War - a war that saw mine clearance operations on a massive scale.

## THE BARRIER THAT NEVER WAS

Allied combat engineers - 'sappers' to give them their time-honoured title - were geared up to play a crucial part in Operation Desert Storm, breaching the defensive perimeter the Iraqis had built around Kuwait from the Gulf to the Iraqi border.

Before the infantry and armoured divisions pressed home their assault, engineers with special tanks had the task of filling ditches with plastic pipes to serve as crossing points, others of laying tank-borne

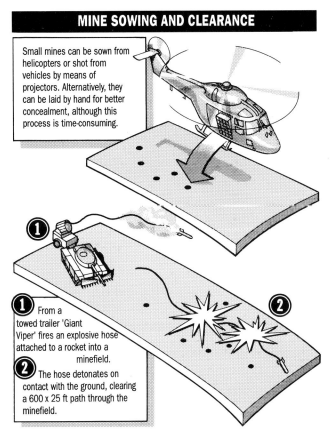

**MINE SOWING AND CLEARANCE**

Small mines can be sown from helicopters or shot from vehicles by means of projectors. Alternatively, they can be laid by hand for better concealment, although this process is time-consuming.

**1** From a towed trailer 'Giant Viper' fires an explosive hose attached to a rocket into a minefield.
**2** The hose detonates on contact with the ground, clearing a 600 x 25 ft path through the minefield.

armoured bridges. Other heavy vehicles were to flatten sand berms and clear paths through the enemy minefields.

In the event, the so-called 'Saddam Line', at first thought to be a formidable obstacle, turned out to be nothing of the sort. Minefields estimated by Allied intelligence as having a depth of 2,000 yards proved to be only 140 yards wide; the 'huge' oil-filled trenches, which the Iraqis were to have set on fire to incinerate assaulting troops, were only six feet across; the sand berms, described by one engineer officer as 'quite pathetic', were poorly constructed and easily breached; defensive bunkers had a flimsy protection of corrugated iron and two layers of sandbags, incapable of withstanding a hit by a mortar bomb.

The Allied combat engineers brought their full arsenal into play at several points of the Saddam Line. The US 1st Infantry Division, nicknamed the 'Big Red One' because of the large figure '1' that forms its insignia, carried out a classic textbook assault on the Iraqi defences to allow the passage of the British 1st Armoured Division through the sand

*The track width mine plough in its raised position. The equipment does not impede an armoured fighting vehicle's fighting ability.*

*The Pathfinder system is used to mark roads through minefields and other dangerous areas. The system can be mounted onto a variety of AFVs.*

and trench fortifications unhindered, and at speed.

First, helicopters lifted squads of reconnaissance troops over the top of the sand berms to form a defensive screen against possible Iraqi counter-attacks. Then, combat bulldozers smashed gaps in the outer sand walls for tanks taking up firing positions in support of the infantry.

Throughout the operation, artillery pounded Iraqi positions to the rear. Combat engineering tractors, towing explosive hose equipment, moved through the breaches in the sand berms made by the M-9 Ace armoured bulldozers and fired their high-explosive charges across the enemy minefields, blasting clear lanes through them. Behind these came engineers on foot, marking safe routes for the British tanks to follow. Bridges of bundled pipes, fascine bridges, were dropped into the anti-tank ditches.

Once the Challenger MBTs had crossed over, the American engineers bulldozed sand over the top of the fascines to make a roadway for the US 1st

Armoured Division's wheeled support vehicles. In all, the 'Big Red One' cut 16 lanes through the berms and minefields over a two-mile front and deployed its own armour and artillery to the north, protecting the flank of the British advance and taking 1,700 prisoners.

Elsewhere on the front it was the same story, with Allied combat engineers punching breaches through the Iraqi defences.

The land war in the Gulf was over in 100 hours. The war of the Allied combat engineers still goes on: minefields are still being cleared, and engineering tasks performed to repair the damage caused by Saddam Hussein's forces. It is tedious, often dangerous work, but the sappers take it in their stride. They always have and they always will.

*A combat dozer fitted to a Challenger I MBT. Note the AFV's grenade launchers on either side of the main armament.*

# CHAPTER NINE

# FROM CATAPULT TO ROCKET

**A**LTHOUGH *the Roman army made wide-spread use of catapults and other stone-throwing devices - including one that could hurl a 112 lb weight over a distance of 400 yards - the first definitely recorded use of artillery in the form that we know it today was at the Battle of Crécy in 1346, when primitive cannon were used to support the impressive firepower of Edward III's archers. Such early weapons were prone to blow themselves apart, and probably killed as many friendly troops as enemy.*

*Throughout the Middle Ages, the development of the artillery weapon depended on parallel discoveries in metallurgy, which allowed the casting of stronger gun barrels, and chemistry, which made gunpowder more stable and reliable. The biggest exponents of artillery during this period were the Turks who, in 1453, during the world's first massed artillery bombardment in the siege of Constantinople, used a 19-ton cannon that could fire a 1,500 lb missile over a range of*

*1,100 yards. After each discharge, it took the gun's crew more than three hours to replace it on its mounting.*

*Mobile artillery was in use early in the 16th century, and in 1512 was used with devastating effect by the French against the Spanish army, exposed on open ground during the Battle of Ravenna. This concept was further refined by King Gustavus Adolphus of Sweden, who supported each of his infantry regiments with light 3-pounder cannon which could be drawn by a single horse or three men; the standard 33-pounder of the day needed up to 25 horses.*

The gunner's task always involved a lot of physical labour. Here, British artilleryman set up a howitzer for action in the First World War.

Canadian artillerymen at gun practice with a 25 pounder gun in the Second World War. This effective artillery piece was standard equipment in the British Army for many years.

*The use of cannon rang the death-knell of walled fortifications. In the English Civil War, many strong castles that had withstood centuries of siege in various wars crumbled under Cromwell's artillery. Over a century later, in 1784, artillery techniques underwent a revolution with the invention, by Henry Shrapnel, of a shell that could be exploded in mid-air, spraying troops with lethal bullets.*

*About the same time, Haider Ali of Mysore used rocket projectiles as an artillery weapon against British forces; the idea was adopted by an Englishman, William Congreve, whose rocket batteries became a firmly-established branch of the artillery during the Napoleonic Wars.*

*Another important milestone in artillery development came in 1851, with the development of a breech-loading cannon by the German firm Krupp.*

*This was quickly followed by the development of a rifled cannon by the English firm Armstrong and Whitworth, and the invention by the Russians of explosive-packed shells that detonated on impact with the target. These three refinements formed the real basis of the modern artillery weapon.*

*By the end of the 19th century, the major armies of the world were using heavy guns with ranges of up to 15,000 yards and field guns with ranges of 9,000 yards, all capable of high rates of fire. Many of these weapons were now fitted with hydraulic shock-absorbing systems to counter recoil, making the task of the gun crews easier.*

*The First World War saw enormous changes in artillery tactics. Firepower was used systematically, under central control, with guns of varying calibres being carefully matched against suitable targets. More protection was provided for the gun crews too, in the form of armoured gun shields, for those weapons positioned in the front line to furnish direct-fire support for the infantry.*

*During the Second World War, British artillery tactics were far in advance of any other by 1943. Much had been learned in the North African campaign, where a single forward observation officer, using radio, could call down the fire of a whole division's artillery on one objective in a matter of minutes. Similar methods were adopted by the Americans.*

*The Russians formed artillery divisions to give concentrated fire prior to an assault, but their system lacked flexibility. The Germans also used concentrated artillery fire, but continued to rely heavily on dive-bombers to achieve what they wanted.*

*Artillery and air power, used in conjunction, are key factors in modern war. Operation Desert Storm underlined that fact. The round-the-clock assault by Allied aircraft severely shook the morale of the Iraqi forces in Kuwait, but it was the massive use of the artillery weapon that finally broke it.*

# ARTILLERY SHELLS Beetles, frogs and other munitions

**M**ANY types of modern artillery shells are rocket-boosted to increase their range by as much as 50 per cent. Heavy artillery pieces can also fire 'smart' artillery missiles such as Martin Marietta's Copperhead or the Acrojet/Avco SADARM (Sense and Destroy Armour) projectile. SADARM ejects several sub-munitions which descend by parachute and use sensors to search for tanks. They attack the tank's more thinly armoured upper surface, achieving a high kill probability.

In the past, the use of artillery against tanks has been of limited effect, accounting for only one per cent of tank kills (but for two-thirds of all battlefield casualties). This is no longer the case. Projectiles such as SADARM are now altering the picture again, and ever-advancing technology will change it further.

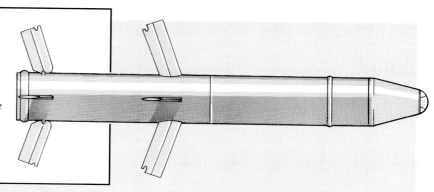

### COPPERHEAD
This projectile follows a ballistic trajectory during the first half of its flight, using four control spines to stabilize it. It then deploys wings and glides while seeking a victim. Copperhead can switch targets in flight and can hit moving objects so long as they are illuminated by ground and airborne laser designators. It is the only US anti-armour weapon which is effective beyond line-of-sight, safe from enemy retaliation. Copperhead has a range of ten miles; the projectile has a 14 lb shaped-charge warhead.

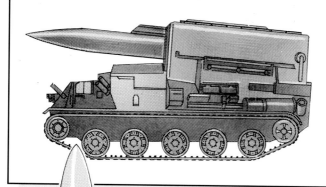

### PLUTON
This French battlefield missile has formed an important part of France's considerable tactical nuclear arsenal since it became operational in 1974. It can be fitted with a number of alternative warheads: the AN51, which has a yield of 25 kilotons (kt), or a 15 kt warhead for use against targets near the front line. Air or ground-burst detonation can be pre-selected. The weapon's range is up to 75 miles. Pluton will be replaced by the Aerospatiale Hades, which will have four times the range and which is due to enter service in 1992.

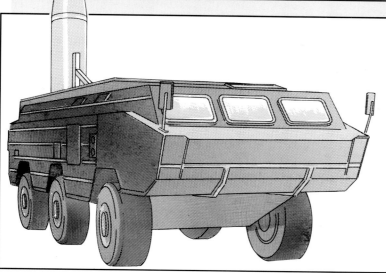

### SS-21 SCARAB
Similar to the US Lance, this Soviet battlefield missile is mounted singly on a 6x6 wheeled vehicle and carries a 1,000 lb warhead over a range of 75 miles. The weapon was designed to carry a 100 kt nuclear warhead, but reports suggest that the standard payload nowadays contains sub-munitions. Inertial guidance is used, making the SS-21 more accurate than the Frog series which it replaces. The Scarab entered service in 1976.

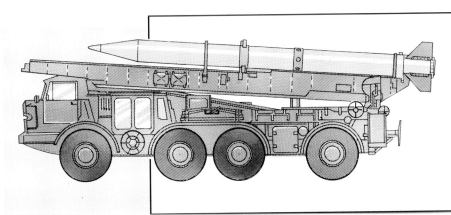

**FROG**

Later variants of the Russian Frog (Free-flight Range Over Ground) unguided tactical missile are in widespread service with several countries, and at least one salvo was fired into northern Saudi Arabia by Iraq during the Gulf War, the missiles falling into open desert. The latest Frog variant, the Frog-7, is carried on a ZIL-135 wheeled vehicle. The 1,000 lb warhead can be either HE or chemical. Its range is about 37 miles.

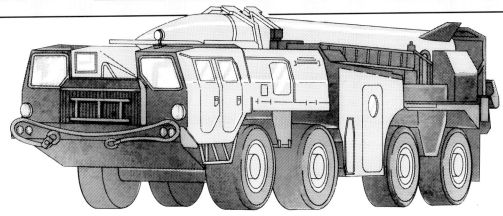

**SS-1C SCUD**

This long-serving Soviet-designed missile became a household word during the Gulf War, when 81 were fired by Iraq at Saudi Arabia and Israel. Most were intercepted by Patriot air-defence missiles or allowed to fall in open country. The first version of the Scud entered Soviet service in 1957 and the mobile SS-1C, mounted on a MAZ-543 transport-launcher, has been used operationally by Egypt as well as Iraq, the Egyptians firing a number of rounds against Israeli positions in Sinai during the Yom Kippur War of 1973. The basic SS-1C Scud-B has a range of 175 miles with a 1,000 lb warhead.

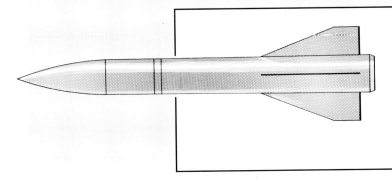

**LANCE**

Developed during the 1960s, this two-stage liquid-fuel led US tactical missile, entered American service in 1972 and since then has formed the backbone of NATO's battlefield nuclear missile inventory. It can be fitted with either a nuclear (10 kt) or conventional warhead, having a rage of 75 miles with the former and 45 miles with the latter. Lance will be replaced by the LTV Army TACMS, which has twice the range and is powered by an advanced solid-propellant rocket meter. TACMS will carry a sub-munitions warhead, but a nuclear-tipped version is under study. This would have a range of 300 miles, just under the 312-mile restriction imposed by the Intermediate Nuclear Forces (INF) Treaty.

**ARTILLERY**

Capable of firing 'smart' munitions, is likely to be a dominant feature of tomorrow's battlefield, especially as it is now combined with advanced fire-control systems. One of the world's most sophisticated gun-laying systems was used in Operation Desert Storm by France's 11th Marine Artillery Regiment, operating in support of the French Daguet Division. Known as Atila, it can track enemy tanks with great accuracy at a range of nearly 20 miles and bring the fire of 155 mm howitzers, the most widely used artillery pieces in the world, to bear. It can also detect a man standing upright at five miles. In addition to its radar equipment, it carries meteorological balloons to gather information on wind speed and direction, temperature and humidity, all of which can affect the trajectories of shells.

# THE BLACK RAIN 'Stalin's Organ' updated

THE Multiple Launch Rocket System (MLRS) is the modern successor to traditional heavy artillery, and far more devastating in terms of firepower. A single MLRS launcher can lay down a weight of fire equivalent to four batteries of 105 or 205 mm howitzers - in other words, 16 heavy guns.

The concept of the MLRS is by no means new. The first successful, albeit primitive, system was the Soviet M-8 Katyusha ('Stalin Organ') of the Second World War, which delivered a salvo of 36 82 mm rockets, each carrying 1 and a half lb of high explosive over a range of just under four miles. The Russians remained at the forefront of multiple-launch battlefield rocket systems until the late 1970s, various developments of the basic Katusha culminating in the BM-27. This is mounted on a ZIL-135 chassis and fires a salvo of 16 220 mm rockets, each carrying a 205 lb high explosive warhead. The system has a range of up to 25 miles and, together with the earlier 40 barrelled BM-21, forms the Soviet Army's standard battlefield rocket artillery equipment.

It was as a counter to the formidable Russian BM-27 that the present-day American MLRS was developed, the intention being from the outset that the system would play a major role in NATO's 'follow-on forces attack' (FOFA) defensive strategy for Northern Europe. This strategy is based on the idea of attacking concentrations of second echelon enemy troops well behind the front line, and so preventing them from reinforcing the leading elements. With a maximum range of over 20 miles, high mobility and the ability to deliver a massive amount of ordnance rapidly and accurately, MLRS was seen as the ideal for this role, in what was always anticipated would be an extremely fast-moving war on NATO's central front.

## MLRS AND ITS TARGETS

The launcher is mounted on a 25-ton tracked vehicle which normally carries a crew of three, but the system can be operated by one man. It carries 12 227mm rockets, each capable of dispensing 644 M77 anti-personnel/anti-tank missiles. These contain a shaped charge that can penetrate armour and then fragment to kill the armoured fighting vehicle's (AFVs) occupants. MLRS can launch single rockets or salvoes, all 12 capable of being launched in under a minute to deliver 7728 bomblets over the target area. How much saturation occurs depends on the range

and other factors such as density of the targets within the selected area.

## GULF WAR OPERATIONS

In Operation Desert Storm, MLRS was used extensively by the US and British Armies during the final phase of the artillery assault against Iraqi positions in Kuwait, prior to the start of the land offensive. The targets were gun batteries, troop and armoured concentrations, most of which were in fixed defensive positions and highly vulnerable to the system's devastating firepower, which earned it the name 'black rain' from the Iraqis. The MLRS units, which have a maximum speed of over 40 mph, moved rapidly from place to place to avoid counter-battery fire. Target information was relayed to the MLRS units by drones which permitted very fast response.

## FUTURE DEVELOPMENTS

A more advanced MLRS, the Phase II, is in its final stages of development. This is designed to

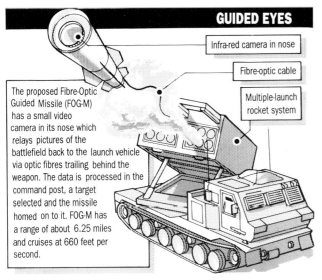

## GUIDED EYES

Infra-red camera in nose

Fibre-optic cable

Multiple-launch rocket system

The proposed Fibre-Optic Guided Missile (FOG-M) has a small video camera in its nose which relays pictures of the battlefield back to the launch vehicle via optic fibres trailing behind the weapon. The data is processed in the command post, a target selected and the missile homed on to it. FOG-M has a range of about 6.25 miles and cruises at 660 feet per second.

developed missile forebody containing three anti-armour terminally-guided sub-munitions (TGSMs). Ejected from the missile over the target area, they independently seek out and attack their own targets.

Accurate delivery of the TGSMs over the target area will depend on information pre-programmed into each MLRS rocket before launch. Once ejected, each sub-munition deploys wings and fins and enters a glide phase, flying on a pre-set trajectory during which it searches for its targets. On detecting a target, the sub-munitions on-board computer checks that it is indeed an AFV, and the TGSM's seeker homes on to it, attacking from above so that its warhead penetrates the tank's thinner top armour.

Another development, now off the drawing board, is FOG-M, a system which uses a fibre-optic cable to guide the projectile towards its intended target.

incorporate a number of different warheads, notably one carrying 28 German-produced AT-2 anti-tank mines. The MLRS Phase III concept, which is intended to be operational by the mid-1990s, is based upon MLRS rockets with a specially

*An MLRS rocket blasts away from its tracked launch vehicle. This system became operational with NATO in 1983.*

# SUPPORTING THE ARMOURED DASH
## Self-propelled artillery that packs the punch

**M**OST artillery nowadays is self-propelled. It has to be, to keep up with fast-moving mechanized units and lend them on-the-spot fire support. Apart from that, self-propelled guns mounted on tracked chassis can operate in terrain that is inaccessible to towed guns, and in an artillery battle they can move quickly from one firing position to another, reducing the danger from enemy counterbattery fire.

At the outset of the Gulf War, the Iraqi Army had some 500 self-propelled guns, mainly 155 mm Soviet-made 251s and 253s. Crewed by five men, these artillery vehicles were capable of firing a 96 lb shell 11 miles, increased to 15 miles with rocket boost. The bulk of the Iraqi artillery force, however, was made up of some 3,000 towed guns, a distinct disadvantage in duels with mobile Allied artillery. For example, when the US 24th Mechanized Infantry Division, one of the spearhead units of XVIII Corps, engaged the Hamurabi Division of the Republican Guard 20 miles west of Basra, the Iraqi armour had very little in the way of self-propelled artillery to support it. The Americans had plenty, and at least six Hammurabi battalions were flattened with artillery fire, including rockets. In another instance, the commander of an Iraqi towed artillery battalion, captured in action, admitted that he had started the battle with 100 guns. After intensive air attacks this figure had been reduced to 80, but when Allied artillery had finished with his command he was left with only seven guns.

The Allied 'armoured punch' in Desert Storm was provided by the US VII Corps, with the US 1st and 3rd and the British 1st Armoured Divisions. The American armour was strongly supported by the 17th, 72nd and 210th Field Artillery Brigades, equipped with the 155 mm M109A2 self-propelled howitzer and multiple rocket launchers. With a crew of six, the M109A2 - the standard NATO self-propelled (SP) gun of this calibre - was able to fire a wide range of munitions out to a 15-mile distance. Also included in the Artillery Brigades' equipment were a number of M110A2 SP howitzers. These 203 mm guns, the heaviest Allied artillery pieces used in the Gulf War, have a crew of 13 and can fire a 200 lb rocket-assisted projectile nearly 17 miles, although a 13-mile range is more normal.

These SP howitzers also provided massive fire support for the British 1st Armoured Division. Within

the Divisional Artillery Group, the 32nd Heavy Regiment had 12 M110s and the 26th Field Regiment 16 M109s; the 4th Armoured Brigade's 2nd Field Regiment and the 7th Armoured Brigade's 40th Field Regiment each deployed 24 M109s. In the softening-up artillery bombardment that preceded the ground assault on Kuwait, the 1st Armoured Division alone fired 2,500 rounds of 203 mm and 10,000 rounds of 155 mm ammunition as part of the greatest barrage unleashed since the Second World War, causing havoc among the Iraqi positions.

On the move, Allied SP artillery commanders engaged in Desert Storm relied heavily on accurate

gunlaying. They were able to receive print-outs of satellite photographs without undue delay, gleaning useful target information from them.

Additionally, a network of navigation beacons was set up throughout the desert, in the vicinity of Kuwait and Southern Iraq, by Allied topographical survey teams.

These consisted simply of oil drums mounted in concrete, with geographic co-ordinates painted on the side. They had been established with great accuracy by the use of the NAVSTAR satellite navigation system and were much used by self-propelled gun batteries setting up new positions.

*The American M109A2 155 mm howitzer is standard NATO equipment. It fires a shell over a range of 15 miles and has a six-man crew.*

Developed by Rockwell International, the NAVSTAR system is designed to provide pinpoint navigational accuracy to land, sea and air forces in the field. It is part of the Global Positioning System and involves a small galaxy of 18 satellites, placed in overlapping orbits and circling the Earth every 12 hours. The GPS system can fix a spot on the ground to within an accuracy of 52 feet.

# CHAPTER TEN

# WAR IN SPACE

THE *flight of an intercontinental ballistic missile (ICBM) comprises a number of events. It begins with the boost phase, which lasts from three to five minutes. During this time, two or three rocket motor stages lift the missile to an altitude of about 125 miles clear of the Earth's atmosphere. Next comes the warhead deployment phase, in which multiple warheads (Multiple Independent Re-entry Vehicles, or MIRVs) leave the main missile in a sequence lasting up to five minutes. Each warhead, there may be up to ten, follows its own ballistic trajectory down through the atmosphere to its target, releasing decoys as it falls to confuse enemy radar and missile defences. MIRVs can be programmed to climb as high as 600 miles above the earth before beginning their re-entry phase. The terminal stage, which is the time between re-entry and the warhead exploding, lasts about two minutes.*

*Multiply this by 2,400, which was roughly the number of land- and sea-launched strategic missiles on the Soviet Union's inventory in the mid-1980s, and the size of the threat becomes apparent. So does the awesome task facing the planners of the US Defense Department's Strategic Defense Initiative (SDI), popularly known as 'Star Wars'.*

*SDI is the biggest defence research effort in American history and has the basic aim of building a defensive system capable of destroying intercontinental ballistic missiles on trajectories from silos in Asia to targets in the USA. It includes several layers of defence, each with the task of destroying as many missiles and warheads as possible at a particular stage of their flight.*

*The first priority is to detect the launch of an ICBM, using specialized surveillance satellites. The next is to compute the trajectories of its warheads, and their likely targets, as well as discriminating between genuine missiles and decoys. Next, defensive weaponry must be precise enough to intercept missile or warhead targets with a 100 per cent certainty of destroying them. This destruction may be achieved by weapons relying on kinetic energy - much the same as the impact of a bullet - or by laser and particle beam weapons.*

The nosecone of an ICBM is slowly lowered over the head of the missile to check its fit.

*Kinetic energy weapons, classed as direct-hit projectiles with no warhead, absorbed much of the early SDI research because they could be developed more cheaply than other systems and brought to an operational standard with existing technology.*

*In June 1984, the so-called 'Homing Overlay Experiment' demonstrated that a projectile fired from a fixed base could destroy an incoming re-entry vehicle outside the Earth's atmosphere. The interceptor missile, made from 'off the shelf' components, homed in on the re-entry vehicle using infra-red sensing and on-board data processing, and then 'killed' it by deploying a circular array of sprung steel blades from its nose cone. The RV impacted on these and was totally destroyed.*

*Kinetic energy weapons being developed under the SDI programme include both interceptor* missiles and hypervelocity gun systems. Primary roles of such systems are mid-course engagement of re-entry vehicles (RVs) not destroyed in the ICBM's boost or post-boost phases, the destruction of RVs that have not deployed all their MIRV warheads, and finally the destruction of any warheads that may have got through and entered their terminal attack phase.

There are problems associated with the use of kinetic energy weapons. The first is that they must be accurate enough to strike incoming RVs at as high an altitude as possible. Modern ICBM warheads have a so-called 'salvage fusing' mechanism that causes them to detonate if they are about to be intercepted by an anti-missile missile. The consequences of a multi-megaton warhead detonating at an altitude of ten miles or even more, would still be catastrophic for the area of ground beneath it.

The real secret of making SDI effective is to destroy enemy ICBMs as soon as possible after launch. Kinetic energy weapons cannot do this, as the elapsed time between launch detection and interception is too long. But there are other weapons, now under development, which can literally strike with the speed of light.

*Above:* A Titan II ICBM in its silo. Together with Minuteman, Titan formed the backbone of America's land-based strategic arsenal.

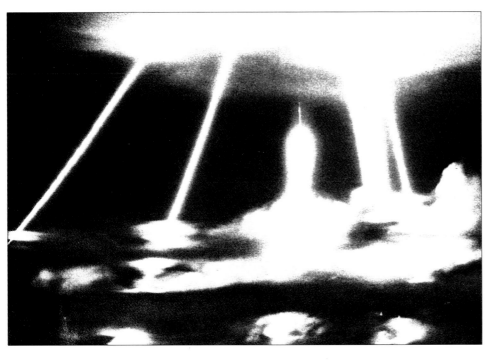

*Left:* MIRVs re-enter the Earth's atmosphere in a spectacular light-show.

# SCI-FI BECOMES REALITY Laser and particle beam weapons

THERE is a distinct difference between laser and particle beam weapons, which are sometimes erroneously classed as one and the same. They are not.

A laser produces a coherent beam of light designed to burn through a target, or at least weaken it to the point where it becomes ineffective, by focusing intense energy on its surface. A particle beam weapon uses the power of a controlled explosion to create enough electromagnetic energy to accelerate and focus a beam of charged atomic particles, either protons or electrons, towards the target. Damage is caused through destructive nuclear reactions triggered when the particles hit the target.

Such weapons perform at the speed of light, 186,000 miles per second. Deployed in space, they could react quickly to any unannounced and potentially hostile missile launch anywhere in the world.

The United States and the Soviet Union have both carried out intensive research into laser and particle beam weapons. America has a tri-service laser test range at the White Sands Missile Range, New Mexico, and the testing of prototype laser weapons is an ongoing process. In 1978, the US Navy destroyed a missile in flight with a laser weapon, and in 1983 the USAF's Airborne Laser Laboratory, a converted Boeing C-135 mounting a prototype laser 'gun', destroyed five Sidewinder missiles launched from another aircraft at ranges of between five and ten miles.

These tests used chemical lasers, which function by

means of a chemical explosion between gases such as hydrogen and fluorine to generate their light beam. They are the only laser systems approaching operational capability, but their drawback is that they require a large amount of fuel and an elaborate array of optics that would be expensive and complex to lift into space.

## X-RAY LASERS
Present-day research is concentrating on a nuclear-pumped X-ray laser systems; this uses a small nuclear explosion to energize a series of metal rods which emit an intense burst of radiation. However, research into chemical lasers as potential ground-based defensive systems continues under a programme called 'Fire Pond' at the Massachusetts Institute of Technology. Research into X-ray lasers is carried out by the Lawrence Livermore Laboratory near San Francisco under a separate programme known as 'Excalibur'.

Yet another research programme, called 'White Horse', is under way at the Los Alamos Scientific Laboratory, and studies the development of particle beam weapons. The ultimate goal is to develop particle beam battle stations, which could be placed in low earth orbit and use a highly focused beam of hydrogen particles against hostile ICBMs in the boost and mid-course phases of their trajectories. Particle beams would not be affected by any 'hardening' an enemy might incorporate in his missiles to protect them from the heat effects of laser weapons.

## SOVIET DEVELOPMENT
The Soviet Union is thought to have invested up to five times as much as the USA in developing laser and particle beam weapons. It has 12 big research centres and six laser test installations, the most important of which is at Sary-Shagan in Kazakhstan. In addition, manufacturing plants for laser weapons have been identified at Troitsk. On another site, the USSR has built a giant pulse laser which is likely to be ready for operational use by the end of the century. In fact, while continually objecting to

*Particle-beam technology under test in a US Navy laser laboratory. Massive energy resources need to be harnessed for this kind of research.*

America's Strategic Defence Initiative, the Soviet Union has been steadily building up its own capability to fight a war in space, starting with a network of communications systems and missile defence systems which can be rapidly deployed in time of crisis.

Even as the danger of confrontation between the super-powers recedes, such systems may have a key role to play in ensuring world peace in the 21st century. The threat of nuclear war is still present,

*The results of the first test-firing of a laser under development with the US Navy were completely successful, as this photograph shows.*

for third-world nations armed with new technology are still racing to develop weapons of mass destruction. The 'Star Wars' defences of both east and west must be prepared to cope with that threat, from whatever direction it might come.

# PATRIOT AND STAR WARS Killing the unfriendly missile

**A**NTI-MISSILE systems, which form the basis of so-called 'Star Wars' programmes, have been around for a long time.

In the 1960s the USA developed a workable anti-ballistic missile (ABM) defensive system called 'Safeguard'. This comprised a long-range ABM called 'Spartan', designed to destroy incoming warheads outside the earth's atmosphere, and a shorter-range backup one called 'Sprint'. The first Safeguard installation was declared operational on 1 October 1975, but was deactivated on the orders of Congress the next day.

This left the Soviet Union as the only nation deploying an anti-ballistic missile system, the ABM-1B Galosh, which is a three-stage solid propellant rocket carrying a nuclear warhead designed to detonate outside the atmosphere. There were originally four sites distributed around Moscow when the system became operational in 1968, but two of these sites were later closed down.

Systems such as Galosh are unwieldy and suitable only for the defence of carefully selected key targets, like capital cities. Both the USA and USSR are now turning their attention to space-based anti-missile systems as a more viable proposition.

## AMERICA'S MOST PUBLIC MISSILE

There is no questioning the usefulness of air defence missiles in countering the threat from tactical ballistic missiles. The Gulf War, with its unforgettable images of Patriot missiles rising like glowing darts to intercept incoming Scuds, demonstrated this with greater eloquence than words.

The Raytheon MIM-104A Patriot was developed to replace the Nike Hercules and Hawk SAM systems, and so form the cornerstone of the US Army's air defence in the field during the 1980s and '90s. The system was designed to intercept high-level and medium altitude targets in the face of heavy countermeasures. Patriot became operational with the US Army in 1985, and in the autumn of 1986 an important milestone in the weapon's capability was reached when a Patriot unit, equipped with modified software, launched an MIM-104 round which successfully intercepted a Lance tactical missile during a trial at the White Sands Missile Range in New Mexico. At the moment of interception, the Lance was about eight miles down-range, descending through 26,000 ft at Mach 3.

The Patriot launching trailer carries four missiles individual canisters, each battery having eight trailers. A phased-array radar seeks, tracks and identifies incoming targets, and also commands and tracks all the Patriots launched by a battery. The MEQ-53 is able to guide five Patriots to five separate targets simultaneously, and monitor 100 tracks.

Patriot uses inertial mid-course guidance with semi-active track-via-missile (TVM) terminal homing. The radar illuminates the target for the missile's passive seeker. The weapon downlinks target data to the battery's engagement control station, which then uplinks guidance commands to the missile via the radar.

Patriot has a range of 45 miles and a maximum reported altitude of 78,000 ft. Its launch weight of 2,015 lb includes a 200 lb high-explosive fragmentation warhead. The solid fuel rocket-motor burns for 11 1/2 seconds, boosting Patriot to a maximum speed of Mach 3.7.

The Patriots initially deployed to Saudi Arabia and Israel in the Gulf War carried the PAC-1 upgrade,

**THE PATRIOT'S STORY**

Patriot missile battery receives a minimum 90-second warning of a Scud attack from a surveillance satellite.

The Patriot is launched. The missile is guided to its target by an MPQ-53 radar which can home five missiles on to five separate targets simultaneously.

Patriot engages the incoming Scud and its proximity fuse detonates, knocking the enemy missile off course.

with modified search and track radar software that made the missile capable of intercepting an incoming SS-1 Scud and knocking it off course, although not necessarily destroying its warhead.

### PATRIOT UPDATED

Later, missiles were deployed with a further upgrade, this time to PAC-2, in which the fuse sensitivity was improved, the missile warhead enlarged and guidance alogrithms upgraded. These changes enable Patriot to destroy a missile warhead travelling much faster, even up to speeds of Mach 8.

41 Scuds were fired at Saudi Arabia and 40 at Israel. These were countered by 130 Patriot launches, most of which found their targets. The remarkable air defence missiles undoubtly played their part in persuading the Israelis not to launch a massive retaliation against Iraq.

Left: *Test-launching of a Patriot missile. Patriot's solid-fuel rocket-motor boosts it to nearly four times the speed of sound.* Below:*A Patriot missile battery in position in the Saudi Arabian desert.*

# THE RING OF CONFIDENCE 'Pebbles' that girdle the earth

**A**BRILLIANT *Pebble does everything. The ultimate concept is for a device sitting up there, floating around. Once it is given a command to go out and do something, it cranks up its own systems, then does its own tracking, homing and interception.'*

Simple words, used by Dr O'Dean Judd, the US Strategic Defense Initiative's chief scientist, to describe an equally simple concept - but one that might provide the ultimate solution to all the problems associated with 'Star Wars' defences.

## SMART ROCKS AND OTHER IDEAS

'Brilliant Pebbles', a concept credited to Dr Lowell Wood of the Lawrence Livermore Laboratories in California, is only the latest in a string of ideas for basing what used to be called 'smart rocks' in space. It involves a constellation of 4,461 independently controlled space-based Interceptors that would hit hostile nuclear missiles soon after launch. In peacetime they would serve as sensor platforms, switching to the interceptor role in a time of crisis.

In SDI spending terms, the cost of the Brilliant Pebbles system would be relatively cheap, about $5,70 billion, with an additional $3 billion for the launch costs. The deployment of such a system

would dramatically reduce the cost of the Phase 1 SDI programme, which is based on the use of kinetic energy weapons. The Pebbles' onboard surveillance and tracking capability means that fewer purpose-built sensor satellites are needed to perform the same function.

If it comes to fruition, and much depends on defence spending cutbacks, as well as technical considerations, the Brilliant Pebbles constellation will be placed in an orbit from which it will provide coverage of the entire planet, poised to counter a missile threat from any point of the globe.

## HOW THEY WORK

The interceptors will be deployed in bunches on low-cost launchers at an orbital altitude of 290 miles, and will react quickly enough to permit interception of missiles before the latter complete the initial 'fast burn' phase of their ascent. The Pebbles will be able to travel hundreds, even thousands of miles to intercept their targets. According to Lowell Wood, the key to successful development rests with the propulsion system, which will enable the vehicle to 'sprint' in any direction to intercept manoeuvring missiles. Each Pebble will be encased in a 'life jacket' which will protect the interceptor's systems throughout its planned ten-year life in Earth orbit.

The Americans envisaged 12 Brilliant Pebbles flight tests as part of the lead-in to full scale development. In order not to contravene the US-Soviet anti-ballistic missile treaty, the first eight were to be sub-orbital and the final four orbital, but with unfuelled interceptors.

The first sub-orbital test, on 25 August 1990, intended to determine whether the sensors for Brilliant Pebbles could detect and track a thrusting rocket motor, ended in failure when telemetry from the Black Brant X rocket booster was lost soon after launch from Wallops Island, Virginia. Both the rocket and its payload fell into the Atlantic Ocean.

## SUCCESS IN ACTION

The experiment did, however, represent one triumph for the SDI programme. The launch was the first to be observed by an orbiting device called the Ultraviolet Plume Instrument, installed in a Defense Department research satellite. The ultraviolet instrument is intended to collect data on the plumes produced by rockets as their engines burn. Such

**ROCKS IN SPACE**

Over 4,500 small satellites girdle the earth in a 290-mile-high orbit.

On command from earth cases open to loose 'thruster interceptors which home in on an enemy missile.

Incoming enemy missile is destroyed by the high energy impact of the interceptor colliding with it.

*An artist's impression of a single Pebble, encased in its protective jacket. Over 4,000 would be placed in orbit.*

data could be used to develop ways of tracking enemy missiles, and aiming US defensive weapons at them.

Brilliant Pebbles testing continues. Justification for the concept depends increasingly on the need for protection against the so-called 'Third World threat', whereby countries with a developing nuclear capability could launch an attack on the United States.

In this context, one of the biggest problems facing SDI planners lies in obtaining accurate intelligence assessments of a particular country's missile programme, and what stage its nuclear technology development might have reached. Poor intelligence had a profound effect on targeting Iraq's missile and nuclear sites during the Gulf War, and only in the aftermath of that conflict was it realized that many nuclear research plants had escaped unscathed. What happened in Iraq could easily be happening elsewhere and the 'Brilliant Pebbles' concept will help to counter that menace.

# PART THREE

# 21ST CENTURY NAVAL POWER

*The Soviet Kara class anti-submarine warfare cruiser is still a menacing sight even by moonlight.*

# CHAPTER ELEVEN

# WINGS OF THE NAVY

**B**Y *the mid-1930s, aircraft carriers featured prominently in the navies of the world's great maritime nations: Britain, the United States and Japan. The Royal Navy, with the greatest number of carriers in service, preferred to deploy them singly with each of its fleets around the world, from the Atlantic to China. The Americans and Japanese, on the other hand, preferred to concentrate their carrier forces and support them with a strong screen of cruisers and destroyers.*

*The Royal Navy was the first to demonstrate the effectiveness of the aircraft carrier in war. On 1st November 1940, Fairey Swordfish torpedo-bombers from the carrier HMS* Illustrious *crippled the Italian battle fleet at Taranto, assuring British naval superiority in the Mediterranean.*

*The lesson was not lost on the Japanese, and on 7 December 1941, aircraft of the Imperial Japanese Navy's fast carrier attack force shattered the US Pacific Fleet at Pearl Harbor. By an amazing stroke of luck, the Pacific Fleet's aircraft carriers were at sea, and escaped unharmed; they were used to form the nucleus of new task forces that eventually took the war to the enemy.*

*Fortunate in its industrial power, the United States built the ships, aircraft and equipment and trained the land, sea and air forces that ultimately beat down the Japanese, drove them from their strategically located island bases, cut off their raw materials, and placed the Allied forces in a position to launch the final air and amphibious offensives against the Japanese Home Islands. These offensives were in the end made unnecessary by the awesome power of the atomic bomb.*

*For the first time in history, naval engagements were fought entirely in the air without opposing surface forces sighting each other.*

*Logistics, in the vast distances of the Pacific Ocean, took on a new importance. Refuelling and replenishment at sea were developed to a high standard and increased the mobility and staying power of fleet forces.*

*In the course of the war, US Navy and Marine pilots destroyed over 15,000 Japanese aircraft in the air and on the ground, sank 174 warships*

Condensation swirls from the propeller tips of a F4U-5N Corsair night-fighter on USS *Boxer* during the Korean War.

HMS *Ark Royal* was the last of the Royal Navy's traditional carriers. She displaced 43,340 tons and was 810 ft long.

totalling 746,000 tons and 447 merchant ships totalling 1,600,000 tons. It was a creditable record, but the Navy's air arm did not play an entirely independent role. It operated as it had developed, as an integral part of naval forces, contributing its full share to the power of the fleet and the achievement of its mission in controlling the sea.

In the Korean War, too, US Navy and British Commonwealth carrier aircraft played a vital role, carrying out a sustained interdiction campaign against enemy targets from the outset. This demonstrated another aspect of the carrier's versatility: its ability to be deployed to any flashpoint at short notice, providing a powerful on-the-spot striking force while land-based air power assembled its resources.

Since then, naval air power has performed a spectacular role in several limited wars, from the Anglo-French operation in Suez, 1956, to the 1991 Gulf War. Without it, Britain could not have succeeded in recapturing the Falkland Islands in 1982. The Russians, too, absorbed the lessons of other navies, and in the 1970s formed a long-range 'blue water' naval force based on carrier task groups.

The whole field of naval aviation was revolutionized, in November 1961, with the commissioning of the world's first nuclear-powered aircraft carrier, the USS Enterprise.

In addition to virtually unlimited high-speed endurance, nuclear propulsion for aircraft carriers provides additional space for aviation fuel and ordnance. The USS Enterprise displaces 83,350 tons fully laden and carries an air group of between 70 and 100 aircraft, according to type. She is overshadowed today by mighty carriers of the improved Nimitz class, which displace 96,836 tons at full load and are over 1,000 ft in length. Such vessels, in their own right, provide a striking force of terrifying power.

Britain's long line of traditional aircraft carriers ended with HMS Ark Royal, which was paid off and broken up in 1979. During her last voyages she operated Phantom and Buccaneer aircraft. She was to have been replaced by a new carrier called CVA-01, which was ordered in July 1963 but cancelled in 1966.

CVA-01 was designed to operate both V/STOL and conventional aircraft. Her 'island' (superstructure) was sited so that aircraft could taxi outboard of it on the starboard side, a radical concept at the time and one that still has a lot of merit.

# THE CARRIER AIR WING  A weapon of awesome power

THE modern, nuclear-powered aircraft carrier would undoubtedly play a decisive part in the outcome of a full-scale war. On average, each US Navy fleet has eight task forces, covering the whole spectrum of warfare from air strike through amphibious assault to submarine attack. At the heart of the whole organization is the Battle Group, usually consisting of two carriers - a nuclear-powered attack carrier of the USS *Nimitz* class, and a smaller attack carrier of the USS *Midway* or *Forrestal* Class.

The interceptor element of a USN Carrier Air Wing (CVW) is provided by two squadrons or Grumman F-14 Tomcats. The variable-geometry Tomcat is powered by two 20,900 lb Pratt & Whitney TF30-P-414A turbofans, which give it a maximum low-level speed of 911 mph (Mach 1.2) and a high-altitude speed of 1,544 mph, or Mach 2.34. It is equipped with the Hughes AN/AWG-9 weapons control system, enabling the two-man crew to detect airborne targets at ranges of up to 170 nautical miles, depending on their size, and small targets such as cruise missiles at 65 nm.

The system can track 24 targets and initiate attacks on six of them at the same time, at a variety of altitudes and ranges. The Tomcat's built-in armament consists of one General Electric M61A1 20 mm Vulcan gun mounted on the port side of the forward fuselage, with 675 rounds. Main missile armament comprises four Sparrow AAM, partly recessed under the fuselage, or four Phoenix AAMs mounted below the fuselage.

The Tomcat can also mount four Sidewinder AAMs, or two Sidewinder plus two Phoenix or two Sparrow, on underwing pylons. Additionally, the F-14 can also carry a mixture of ordnance - missiles or bombs - up to a maximum of 14,500 lb, alongside an array of ECM equipment.

## HORNETS PROVIDE THE STING

The Carrier Air Wing's strike element comprises two squadrons of Macdonnell Douglas F/A-18 Hornets and one squadron of Grumman A-4E Intruders. The F-18 Hornet is the fighter-interdictor variant, while the F/A-18's role is ground attack. Both are single-seaters and are powered by two General Electric F404 turbofans developing 16,000 lbs of thrust.

The Hornet's equipment includes a Hughes APG-6S radar with air-to-air and air-to-ground modes, external sensors include laser tracker and FLIR pods. The aircraft carries the AIM-120 air-to-air missile in the interceptor role and a wide array of ground-attack weaponry, including the infra-red Maverick air-to-surface missile.

The Intruder, designed specifically as a carrier-based low-level attack bomber, saw extensive service over Vietnam and repeated its excellent performance in the Gulf War.

Each aircraft can carry up to 15,000 lb of bombs and uses a Digital Integrated Attack Navigation System. This enables the crew to preselect an attack pattern for the aircraft, which leaves the target area under automatic control after weapons release. The CVW also has a squadron of KA-6D flight refuelling

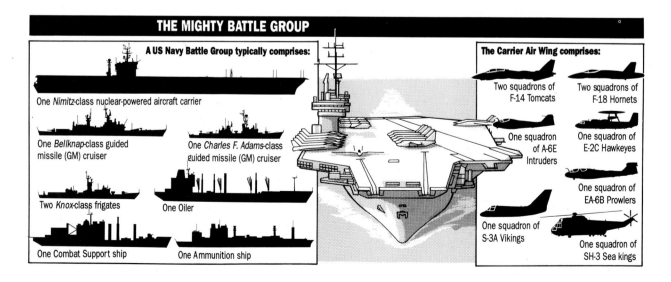

**THE MIGHTY BATTLE GROUP**

A US Navy Battle Group typically comprises:

One *Nimitz*-class nuclear-powered aircraft carrier

One *Bellknap*-class guided missile (GM) cruiser

One *Charles F. Adams*-class guided missile (GM) cruiser

Two *Knox*-class frigates

One Oiler

One Combat Support ship

One Ammunition ship

The Carrier Air Wing comprises:

Two squadrons of F-14 Tomcats

Two squadrons of F-18 Hornets

One squadron of A-6E Intruders

One squadron of E-2C Hawkeyes

One squadron of EA-6B Prowlers

One squadron of S-3A Vikings

One squadron of SH-3 Sea kings

tanker, and one of the electronic warfare version of the Intruder, the EA-6B Prowler.

Completing the line-up is a squadron of Grumman E-2C Hawkeye early warning and control aircraft, a squadron of Lockheed S-3A Vikings and one of SH-3H Sea King helicopters. The two latter squadrons operate jointly in the anti-submarine role.

## WILL THE FUTURE HAPPEN?

Future US Navy Carrier Air Wings may be equipped with an advanced tactical fighter aircraft, the General Dynamics/McDonnell Douglas A-12. This is to be powered by two F404 engines and will provide a two-seat subsonic stealthy attack capability. The US Navy has a requirement for 620 A-12s to replace its A-6 Intruders. The A-12 programme has been subjected to delays and cutbacks, but the aircraft - provisionally named the Avenger II - will be vital to the Navy's future efficiency.

For many years the Soviets had considered the threat of the west's carrier aircraft, bearing nuclear devices, to be a danger to the Russian landmass, and for a long time they lagged behind in the development of a maritime fleet. Their ambitions perhaps, did not run to 'blue water' operations. But all this has now changed.

Glasnost or not, the Soviet Navy continues to develop its own air power, which will soon be boosted by a new generation of V/STOL fighters to operate from existing *Kiev*-class carriers, and the entry into service of three large nuclear attack carriers operating advanced conventional take-off and landing aircraft. Already the west is glimpsing new aspects of the Soviet's programme with the unveiling of a new YAK V/STOL aircraft at the 1990 Paris Air Show. The threat at sea will still exist in the 21st century.

These three vessels, the *Tbilisi, Riga* and *Ulyanovsk,* will have the priority task of maintaining air superiority over and around Soviet nuclear-submarine bases, as well as undertaking 'blue water' operations as part of a western-style battle group in which they will be supported by battlecruisers, cruisers and destroyers, all of them heavily armed against surface and air attack.

With forces such as this, the USSR will have a choice: either to challenge the USA's dominance of the sea, or join forces with America in the role of world peacemaker.

*The LTV A-7 Corsair II is still used by the USN and the USMC, but is being replaced by the Hornet. Here a USN Corsair is being armed with Sidewinders for a CAP in the Red Sea during Operation Desert Shield.*

# THE EYES OF THE FLEET  Naval early warning

**T**HE aircraft that has formed the mainstay of the US Navy's airborne early warning capability for many years is the Grumman E-2 Hawkeye, the prototype of which first flew on 20 October 1960. The first 20 E-2As were used for service evaluation and carrier trials, and the type was formally accepted into US Navy service on 19 January 1964, when it began to equip Early Warning Squadron VAW-11 at San Diego. This unit went to sea with its Hawkeyes aboard the USS *Kitty Hawk* in 1966, by which time a second squadron, VAW-12, had also been formed.

Sixty-two E-2As were built, including the prototypes, and construction ended early in 1967. The E-2B, which flew in February 1969, had a number of refinements including an L-304 micro-electronic computer, and all operational E-2As were subsequently updated to E-2B standard.

## RADAR UPDATES

The latest Hawkeye variant, and the one in service today, is the E-2C, the first of two prototypes flying in January 1971. The earlier model Hawkeyes had been equipped with the General Electric APS-96 search and tracking radar, which even in its original form was capable of automatic target detection and tracking over water.

To achieve this, a technique called airborne moving target indication (AMTI) was introduced to suppress unwanted echoes from the sea. The APS-96 equipped E-2A and B were designed for 'blue water' operations far from land, but early operational experience - particularly in the Vietnam War - showed that the Hawkeye could be required to operate close to land and to detect targets against ground clutter. This posed problems for the APS-96, and in 1965 the US Navy began trials with a modified radar, the APS-111. Further trials and modifications to reject unwanted ground signals resulted in a new radar, the APS-120, which was capable of target detection and tracking over both sea and land.

This system was fitted in the E-2C, and over the years further improvements have resulted in the production of new radar models, the latest of which is the APS-145. This will replace the APS-139 system which currently equips the US Navy's Hawkeye fleet.

The APS-145 really gets to grips with the problems of ground clutter, using a technique called 'environmental processing' to eliminate almost totally

radar 'false alarms' produced, say, by fast motorway traffic. The overland performance of the new radar, comment its manufacturers, is close to that of the Boeing E-3 AWACS' surveillance radar. The APS-145 also extends the Hawkeye's detection range to 350 miles, countering the threat presented by aircraft armed with long-range Cruise missiles.

The E-2C Hawkeye carries a crew of five and, in addition to the US Navy, has also been supplied to Egypt, Israel, Japan and Singapore.

A US Navy Hawkeye squadron usually comprises five aircraft, their task being to patrol a task force at a radius of about 200 nautical miles, their radar searching for hostile targets at all levels from the sea up to 100,000 ft. Standing off from the task force at a

*A Grumman E-2C Hawkeye launching from a US aircraft carrier. The aircraft is dominated by its big, saucer-shaped radome.*

range of between 50 and 100 nm on the threat side, the Hawkeye can track up to 200 targets simultaneously, and provide automatic directions to defending F-14 Tomcat fighters via data link, assigning targets in order of threat priority. In war or a real threat situation, one Hawkeye would be airborne over the fleet 24 hours a day. The E-2C also has a valuable secondary role in directing aircraft recovering to their carrier in bad weather.

## HOW THE BRITS DO IT

The Royal Navy suffered from a serious lack of early warning aircraft during the 1982 Falklands War. The RN's last fixed-wing AEW aircraft was the Fairey Gannet AEW3, which was retired in 1979 on the de-

commissioning of Britain's last conventional 'flat top', HMS *Ark Royal*. As a result, picket ships had to be deployed off the Falklands to provide a defensive radar screen, and it was while acting in this role that the destroyer HMS *Sheffield* was hit and disabled by an Argentine Exocet missile. The gap has since been filled to some extent by the deployment of Sea King helicopters fitted with the Thorn EMI Searchwater surveillance radar, mounted in a retractable radome on its starboard rear fuselage.

# STRIKE IN ALL WEATHERS The Intruder's mission

THE Grumman A-6 Intruder has been the US Navy's primary carrier-borne bomber for three decades. Designed specifically to deliver both nuclear and conventional warloads with high accuracy in all weathers, it was one of 11 competitors in a US Navy design contest of 1957, and was selected as the winner on 31 December that year. In March 1959 a contract was placed for four aircraft, followed by four more in 1960, and the A-6A prototype flew on 19 April 1960. The first operational aircraft entered service with Navy Squadron VA-42 on 1 February 1963, and the last A-6A delivery took place in December 1969, by which time 469 had been built.

The A-6A saw extensive action over Vietnam, providing the US Seventh Fleet with a formidable striking force. For the first time in the Vietnam War, the Americans had an aircraft with an advanced avionics weapon system. It was the only operational aircraft that possessed a self-contained all-weather bombing capability, permitting its use in the monsoon season, not only in South Vietnam but also in Laos and in the heavily defended environment of North Vietnam.

### UP-FRONT REVOLUTION

It revolutionized night and all-weather close support techniques when operating with US Marine ground forces, whose forward air controllers (FACs) deployed small radar beacons known as RABFACs. With these, the precise position of a FAC could be displayed on the A-6A's radar scope. The FAC could provide the bearing and distance of a target from the beacon, plus the elevation difference between the two; the bombardier-navigator in the A-6A could enter this data into the weapon system computer and bomb the target in bad weather or at night with an accuracy that could only be achieved by other strike aircraft in broad daylight.

In the hostile environment of North Vietnam, Intruders operated singly against high-value targets or used their advanced avionics to guide other attack aircraft.

On one particularly difficult mission, flown on the night of 30 October 1967 by an Intruder of VA-196 against a vital railway target in Hanoi, the crew (Lt Cdr Charles B. Hunter and Lt Lyle F. Bull) had to evade no fewer than 16 surface-to-air missiles, as well as a fearsome concentration of AAA. Hunter avoided the first salvo of SAM by barrel-rolling the Intruder with 9,000 lb of bombs under its wings, an extremely dangerous manoeuvre and one that testified to the ruggedness of the aircraft. It also kept the aircraft on course for the target, so that Lt Bull could continue to compute his attack pattern. By this time, the AAA fire was so heavy that it lit up the countryside, so much so that Lt Cdr Hunter could see details on the ground. During the final run to the target Hunter stayed right down 'on the deck'. At one point five SAMs were heading for him but each one exploded directly overhead, filling the cockpit with an orange glow and making the aircraft shudder. Despite all the opposition, Hunter and Bull bombed the target accurately and returned safely to their carrier, the USS *Constellation*.

The latest version of the Intruder is the A-6E,

*About to catapult off a crowded and mist-shrouded carrier deck during Operation Desert Storm, the Intruder is ready to fly in all weathers.*

which was developed as a result of technical problems experienced with the A-6A. The new variant featured a Norden APQ-148 multi-mode radar which, although reliable, had a restriction in that the

*The A-6 Intruder is one of the word's most combat-provan aircraft, having seen action over Vietnam, Libya and Iraq.*

Intruder had to be virtually on top of a target before the latter could be positively identified.

To overcome this limitation, the Target Recognition and Attack Multisensor (TRAM) was developed by Hughes Aircraft. This comprises an under-nose turret housing a FLIR sensor plus a laser spot tracker, rangefinder and designator. The A-6E Intruder first flew in March 1974, and the system entered service in 1979. All Intruders are now TRAM-capable.

Intruders played a prominent part in America's punitive strike on targets in Libya in April 1986, and also in the Gulf War. In the initial air strike phase of Desert Storm, they joined with F-15E Strike Eagles in precision attacks on high-priority targets such as nuclear and chemical research centres, power stations and fuel facilities. Later, they undertook a considerable amount of ground-attack work, and were responsible for much of the destruction wrought on retreating Iraqi forces in the Mutlah Gap during the final phase of the Allied ground offensive against Iraq.

An improved version of the Intruder, the A-6F was recently cancelled because of financial constraints, but the Gulf War has undoubtedly given impetus to the programme for upgrading the A-6E. Changes include new computer equipment.

# THE AIR WING'S POTENT FIST  Striking down the enemy

GERMANY was the first nation to use air-launched missiles in an anti-shipping role. In 1943-4, the Germans inflicted considerable losses on Allied shipping in the Mediterranean through using two types of missile: the Henschel HS 293 and the Ruhrstahl AG Fritz-X. The first of these was rocket-powered, and the second a controlled free-fall missile.

Towards the end of the Second World War, when the Allies had gained air superiority, they caused prohibitive losses among the Dornier Do 217 launch aircraft, and the two missile types were switched to land targets, mainly on the Russian Front.

The Korean War produced an urgent US Navy requirement for a precision air-to-surface weapon capable of being launched by carrier-borne aircraft. The result was the Martin Bullpup, a supersonic rocket-powered weapon with a 10-mile range and a 250 lb warhead. It was in widespread use during the 1960s with the US Navy and several other countries,

including the United Kingdom. In terms of range and striking power, air-launched naval missiles have come a long way since Bullpup. Some of the vast array of missiles that are now available are described and illustrated below.

The modern anti-ship missile has in recent years become the weapon with which small nations can challenge larger ones to great effect. The events of 1982 - the Falklands War - brought this home.

One of them, the French built Exocet, has a name which still strikes fear into the hearts of naval crews. It was the Exocet missile, that strapped onto Argentine Skyhawk's, attacked and sank HMS *Sheffield* during the Falklands conflict. It is one of the most widely used of all Western anti-ship missiles.

It is certain that these types of missile will be seen a lot more in the years to come and from that point of view, a close study of armament lists could well reveal some chilling facts, especially when the lists are matched to politically unstable regimes in which the weaponry is found.

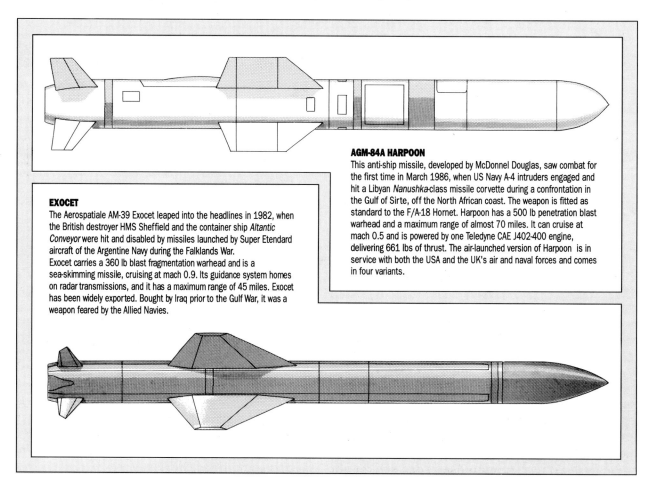

**AGM-84A HARPOON**
This anti-ship missile, developed by McDonnel Douglas, saw combat for the first time in March 1986, when US Navy A-4 intruders engaged and hit a Libyan *Nanushka*-class missile corvette during a confrontation in the Gulf of Sirte, off the North African coast. The weapon is fitted as standard to the F/A-18 Hornet. Harpoon has a 500 lb penetration blast warhead and a maximum range of almost 70 miles. It can cruise at mach 0.5 and is powered by one Teledyne CAE J402-400 engine, delivering 661 lbs of thrust. The air-launched version of Harpoon is in service with both the USA and the UK's air and naval forces and comes in four variants.

**EXOCET**
The Aerospatiale AM-39 Exocet leaped into the headlines in 1982, when the British destroyer HMS Sheffield and the container ship *Altantic Conveyor* were hit and disabled by missiles launched by Super Etendard aircraft of the Argentine Navy during the Falklands War.
Exocet carries a 360 lb blast fragmentation warhead and is a sea-skimming missile, cruising at mach 0.9. Its guidance system homes on radar transmissions, and it has a maximum range of 45 miles. Exocet has been widely exported. Bought by Iraq prior to the Gulf War, it was a weapon feared by the Allied Navies.

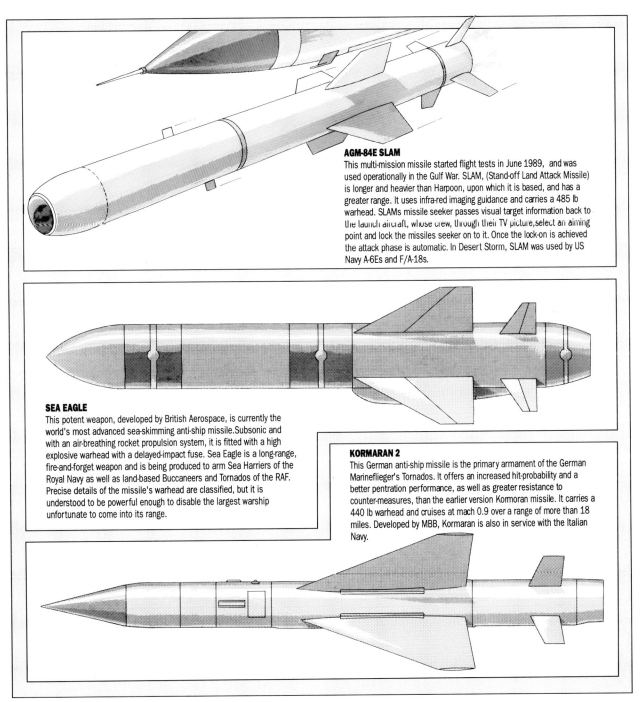

**AGM-84E SLAM**

This multi-mission missile started flight tests in June 1989, and was used operationally in the Gulf War. SLAM, (Stand-off Land Attack Missile) is longer and heavier than Harpoon, upon which it is based, and has a greater range. It uses infra-red imaging guidance and carries a 485 lb warhead. SLAMs missile seeker passes visual target information back to the launch aircraft, whose crew, through their TV picture, select an aiming point and lock the missiles seeker on to it. Once the lock-on is achieved the attack phase is automatic. In Desert Storm, SLAM was used by US Navy A-6Es and F/A-18s.

**SEA EAGLE**

This potent weapon, developed by British Aerospace, is currently the world's most advanced sea-skimming anti-ship missile.Subsonic and with an air-breathing rocket propulsion system, it is fitted with a high explosive warhead with a delayed-impact fuse. Sea Eagle is a long-range, fire-and-forget weapon and is being produced to arm Sea Harriers of the Royal Navy as well as land-based Buccaneers and Tornados of the RAF. Precise details of the missile's warhead are classified, but it is understood to be powerful enough to disable the largest warship unfortunate to come into its range.

**KORMARAN 2**

This German anti-ship missile is the primary armament of the German Marineflieger's Tornados. It offers an increased hit-probability and a better pentration performance, as well as greater resistance to counter-measures, than the earlier version Kormoran missile. It carries a 440 lb warhead and cruises at mach 0.9 over a range of more than 18 miles. Developed by MBB, Kormaran is also in service with the Italian Navy.

The Chinese People's Republic is emerging as a leading exporter of anti-ship missiles. The air-breathing HY-4 missile, developed from the earlier Silkworm used by Iraq in the Gulf War, is thought to have a cruise speed of about Mach 1. The C601 and the C801 are much more advanced; the former is powered by a liquid propellant rocket and is a sea-skimmer, using a monopulse radar seeker for terminal homing, while the C801 is supersonic and carries a 360 lb HE warhead. The C601 is launched by the Chinese Air Force's Tu-16 aircraft and has a range of 100 miles, while the 25-mile-range C801 is carried by the Q-5 supersonic attack aircraft.

The missile will also be the main armament of a new class of 4,000 ton warships to be built for the Chinese Navy.

# CHAPTER TWELVE

# IN DEFENCE OF THE FLEET

ON *21 August 1917, the German Zeppelin L23 was shot down in flames over the North Sea by a Sopwith Pup biplane of the Royal Naval Air Service, flown by Flight Sub-Lieutenant B A Smart. He had taken off from a wooden platform fitted over the forward gun turret of the cruiser HMS* Yarmouth. *After the interception he ditched in the sea and was picked up safely, although the Pup was lost.*

*Smart was awarded the Distinguished Service Order, and assured of a place in history. It was the first time that an enemy aircraft had been destroyed by a fighter launched from a ship at sea.*

*Although the Royal Navy held a commanding lead in aircraft carrier development in the 1920s, it was not to last. Both the USA and Japan were building vessels which, in terms of performance and capacity, would soon outstrip their British counterparts. So would the performance of their carrier-based aircraft. The British also lagged behind in the development of fighters to defend the fleet, giving priority to gunnery spotting aircraft and torpedo-bombers. The British Admiralty was also hampered by the fact that the RAF controlled the Fleet Air Arm until May 1939, when it reverted to the Navy.*

*When the Fleet Air Arm went to war in 1939, the defence of the fleet rested on a few squadrons of Gloster Sea Gladiators, the naval variant of the RAF's last biplane fighter. At that time the Imperial Japanese Navy's fighter squadrons were already equipped with the Mitsubishi A5M monoplane, which would be replaced by the formidable A6M Zero by the time Japan entered the war in December 1941, and the Americans were developing the excellent little Grumman F4F Wildcat.*

*Apart from the Blackburn Roc, an unsuccessful concept which was armed with a four-gun turret and which equipped only two land-based squadrons, the Royal Navy had no purpose-built fighter during the early war years.*

*Its first fighter monoplane, the Fairey Fulmar, was developed from the Battle light bomber, while the Sea Hurricane and Seafire were naval conversions of the two famous RAF fighters. The Fairey Firefly two-seat Fleet fighter was an effective design, but did not enter service until 1944. The Royal Navy filled the fighter gap by purchasing well-proven American types - the F4F Wildcat (named Martlet in RN service), the F6F Hellcat and the Chance Vought F4U Corsair. The Hawker Sea Fury, a powerful fighter that came too late for service in the Second World War, saw action over Korea and destroyed a number of MiG-15 jets.*

The Grumman F4-J Wildcat bore the brunt of the US Defence operations in the Pacific during the early months of the Second World War. Here a Wildcat is ready to take off from USS *Yorktown*.

Although the British were the first to land a jet aircraft on a carrier, when a de Havilland Vampire flown by Lt Cdr E M Brown touched down on the deck of HMS Ocean on 3 December 1945, the Americans quickly seized the lead in the development of naval jet fighters, and never lost it. The F2 Banshee and F9F Panther of Korean War vintage soon gave way to more advanced aircraft like the supersonic Grumman F11F Tiger and the McDonnell F-4 Phantom, arguably the best naval fighter design of all time, given the technology of its day.

In the 1960s the Phantom was also purchased by the Royal Navy, whose squadrons were still equipped with subsonic fighters like the de Havilland Sea Vixen and the Supermarine Scimitar.

In the mid-1970s the US Navy's fighter squadrons began re-equipping with the Grumman F-14 Tomcat, a powerful, heavily-armed long-range interceptor which still forms the backbone of the USN's Fleet defense system

A de Havilland Sea Vixen approaches to land on HMS *Hermes*. In 1982, *Hermes* was the flagship of the Falklands Task Force, operating V/STOL Sea Harriers.

today. The Royal Navy, for its part, was pursuing the vertical take-off path with the British Aerospace Sea Harrier, combined with a new class of light aircraft carrier.

The Soviet Navy was pursuing a similar policy with its Kiev-class carriers and Yak-38 Forger V/STOL aircraft, a combination that came as an unpleasant surprise to NATO observers when it first appeared in 1976.

The Forger was not the last of Russia's surprises. In 1991 the Soviet Union revealed the Yak-141, a supersonic advanced short take-off/vertical landing aircraft that will provide maritime air defence for the Soviet Navy's new large attack carriers. The aircraft will add a new and potent dimension to Soviet power at sea.

# GRUMMAN'S BIG CAT Anytime, anywhere...

**A** DAY in the life of an aircraft carrier is a busy one. The Carrier Air Wing's complement of aircraft operate in a series of launch cycles; these are planned around a basic period of 1 hour 45 minutes, which is the average time between launch and recovery for the shorter-endurance aircraft.

The first wave to launch will recover and land just after the second wave launches, and so on. Longer endurance aircraft like the S-3 Viking and E-3 Hawkeye fly a double cycle of three and a half hours.

In the busy launch cycle of a carrier such as the USS *Nimitz,* the Grumman F-14 Tomcats of the Air Wing's interceptor element are usually away first, providing combat air patrols over the remainder of the launch programme. If the alert state is high prior to launch, the Tomcat crews will remain strapped into their cockpits for anything up to two hours, with all external units plugged into the aircraft, before being positioned on the launch catapults.

## BARRIER, TASK FORCE AND TARGET

An Air Wing's Tomcats are normally tasked to fly three types of mission: Barrier CAP, Task Force CAP and Target CAP.

Barrier CAP involves putting up a defensive screen at a considerable distance from the task force under the direction of a Hawkeye command and control aircraft. Since fighters flying Barrier CAPs are likely to encounter the greatest number of incoming enemy aircraft, Tomcats usually carry their full armament of six Phoenix AAMs. These weapons, which carry a 132 lb warhead, reach a speed of more than Mach 5 and have a range of about 100 miles, which makes them highly suitable for long-range interception of aircraft flying at all levels, and also of sea-skimming Cruise missiles.

Hostile aircraft or missiles that survive the attentions of the Tomcats on Barrier CAP are engaged by the F-14s of the Task Force CAP, which operate within sight of their ships and are armed with a mixture of Phoenix, Sparrow and Sidewinder AAMs. If targets still show signs of breaking through and all defensive AAMs are expended, the F-14s can continue their engagement with their Vulcan cannon at close range.

Target CAP is an escort task, with the Tomcats riding shotgun on the Carrier Air Wing's strike force. For this, the Tomcats' primary armament is the medium- and close-range Sparrow and Sidewinder, backed up by the M61 cannon. In the escort role, the aircraft usually operate in the 'loose pair' battle formation.

## STRIKE ONE, AND ONLY ONE

Because of the lack of Iraqi air opposition, US Navy F-14 Tomcats scored only one air-to-air success in the Gulf War, when an F-14A of Navy Squadron VF-1 (USS *Ranger*) destroyed an enemy helicopter with an AIM-9 Sidewinder, on 6 February 1991. However, the Tomcat's weapon system has shown its prowess on a number of occasions in the Mediterranean area, when CAP fighters have engaged Libyan aircraft presenting a threat to US naval forces.

On one occasion - 19 August 1981 - two Tomcats flown by Cdr Henry Kleeman and Lt Lawrence Muczynski, of Navy Squadron VF-41 (USS *Nimitz*), were flying a CAP over the Gulf of Sirte in north Africa. They were attacked by two Libyan Su-20 Fitters, one of which unsuccessfully fired an Atoll air-to-air missile. Both aircraft had broken hard left, and now Kleeman saw the lead Fitter, the one that had fired the Atoll, enter a climbing left-hand turn toward Muczynski and pass through the loop of the American's maximum-rate turn, still climbing.

As his wingman rolled out of the turn and went after the lead Libyan Fitter, Kleeman reversed his own turn, rolling out to the right in pursuit of the enemy wingman. He waited ten seconds until his target had crossed the sun, then fired an AIM-9L Sidewinder from a range of about 1,300 yards. The missile struck the Fitter in the tailpipe area, causing the Libyan pilot to lose control. He promptly ejected within five seconds.

Muczynski, meanwhile, had also fired a Sidewinder from about 800 yards, and this too destroyed its target. The pilot of the second Fitter was not seen to eject. The time from the first radar contact to the kills taking place was under 60 seconds.

The two Fitters had been destroyed by a combination of superior tactics, superior weapons and vastly superior aircraft. From the moment they had first been detected by the Tomcats' radar, the Libyans had stood little chance of inflicting any damage on their opponents.

In close-in combat, the Tomcat has the advantage of being a very manoeuvrable aircraft, thanks to its automatic, variable-geometry wing, which can be

swept from 20° in the fully forward position to 68°. Another factor is that the F-14 has a long tunnel under the fuselage between the engines, which produces a lifting effect. Tomcat pilots swear that nothing will out-turn them except a Harrier - and Harriers do not fight fairly.

*A Grumman F-14 Tomcat, wings in the fully forward position for low-speed flight, joins the circuit prior to landing on its carrier.*

# THE JUMP JET GOES TO SEA  Harriers and Hawks

**W**E *could see the awful sight of the ships burning at Bluff Cove. The smoke was pouring out, thick and oily, and the entire after section of the ship (Sir Galahad) was glowing red with the heat. It was about 1800 hours and getting dark when we noticed some Skyhawks having a go at some landing craft coming down from the direction of Goose Green. Dave Morgan rolled upside down and pulled hard for the surface.*

*'I followed him down very fast, but he was nearly disappearing in the gloom. It was very hard to keep an eye on him. I slammed the throttle to full power and aimed in the general direction in which Dave had by now disappeared. He must have been about half a mile ahead of me. My air speed was just over 600 knots when I saw two bright flashes from the direction of Dave's aircraft - he had fired both Sidewinders. I watched the white smoke trails and they ended in two fireballs as the Skyhawks disintegrated and hit the sea.*

*'Now where had he got to? Fortunately he opened up on the other two Skyhawks with his cannon and I just flew towards the shell splashes in the water - there he was. As I approached for an attack Dave was in the way, but fortunately pulled out and cleared from my sights. I pointed the missile at the nearest bogey and heard the growl in my ears as the missile acquired him. I fired, thinking he was too far*

*and going too fast for the missile to get him. The range was two or two-and-a-half miles, and as I watched the Sidewinder's trail, it seemed to me that it flamed out about 300 yards short of its target. Evidently it did not, as there was a blinding flash, followed fractions of a second later by the Skyhawk impacting on the ground.'*

This action took place on 8 June 1982. It was fought by Lt Dave Smith, RN, and Flt Lt Dave Morgan, RAF, both of No 800 Squadron of the Fleet Air Arm, operating from the carrier HMS *Hermes*, and it was the squadron's last combat of the Falklands War.

### THE JET THAT JUMPED FROM THE SEA
The aircraft they flew was the British Aerospace Sea Harrier FRS 1, which was also operated by No 701 Squadron aboard HMS *Invincible*, and by Nos 809 and 899 Squadrons, whose Sea Harriers were divided between both aircraft carriers. No 809 Squadron had been specially activated for the Falklands War operation and was very quickly

*The Sea Harrier FRS 2 has greatly enhanced the type's combat effectiveness. This artist's impression shows the AIM-120 armament. Existing FRS 1s are being upgraded to FRS 2 standard.*

**LOITERING WITH INTENT**

The Sea Harrier flies a figure-of-eight combat air patrol pattern. Endurance depends on the distance from the parent carrier or shore base. Patrols are carried out with pairs of aircraft.

The CAP pair is under the control of an air defence vessel up to 60-80 miles distant, which is protected by 'stand-off patrols' and its own missile defences.

prepared in order to be ready for action against any contingency.

From the start, the primary task of the Sea Harrier squadrons was fleet air defence. Combat air patrols were carried out in increasing numbers each day as the British Task Force came closer to the Falklands. CAPs were flown at between 60 and 80 miles from the British ships, and during the approach to the Total Exclusion Zone, which the British government had set up for 200 nautical miles around the Islands, a good deal of night flying took place.

When the action began, the combination of V/STOL Sea Harrier and AIM-9L Sidewinder missile proved a deadly one. The 28 Sea Harriers deployed with the Task Force destroyed 20 Argentine aircraft and probably destroyed three more, which was no mean achievement under the vile operating conditions of the South Atlantic winter, and given the fact that the aircraft's Blue Fox air intercept radar had limited capabilities.

Aircraft were steered towards incoming raiders by radar air defence ships like HMS *Brilliant*. Pilots then mostly had to rely on their eyesight to locate the attackers, which were almost always at low level. The Sea Harriers overcame problems of distances too. At times, their two aircraft carriers were stationed up to 250 miles east of the Falklands, which meant that for every two Sea Harriers on CAP, another pair would be returning to their ship, and a third pair on the way out. Three CAP stations were normally maintained, so with 18 aircraft needed to patrol those areas, full CAP was only achieved because of the Sea Harrier's excellent serviceability

record, which was a remarkable 95 per cent.

At the height of the campaign, on 21 May 1982, when British forces went ashore at San Carlos, Sea Harriers were being launched on CAPs at the rate of a pair every 20 minutes. No Sea Harrier was lost in air-to-air action.

**A LEGACY THAT LIVES ON**

The Sea Harrier's achievement in the Falklands War was summed up by Lt Cdr Nigel 'Sharkey' Ward, commanding No 801 Squadron:

*'One frequent comment has been that the enemy aircraft had too little fuel to remain in the target area for more than a few minutes. This was obviously not the case, as any student of Mirage and A-4 Skyhawk performance figures can easily establish. They had almost as much loiter time available over the target as did the Sea Harrier and, most importantly, they had the considerable advantage of being on the offensive and with vastly superior numbers... The Argentines christened Sea Harrier* La Muerte Negra - *the Black Death - and publicized this fact in their national radio broadcasts. They lived in fear of the Fleet Air Arm, though to their credit they continued with their almost suicidal offensive against our land and naval forces until Port Stanley fell.'*

The Royal Navy now has a new generation of Sea Harrier, the FRS 2, which is equipped with the Blue Vixen pulse-doppler radar and other advanced avionics. It is armed with the AIM-120 Advanced Medium-Range Air-to-Air Missile (AMRAAM) and incorporates many features of the AV-8B/Harrier GR 5, including the HOTAS system.

# THE TASK FORCE'S 'GOALKEEPERS'
## Cruising the world's oceans

THE modern naval cruiser bears little relationship to its ancestor of the Second World War. Then, the cruiser's role was to act as the eyes of the fleet; it was fast and carried an armament which, in theory at least, would allow it to fight its way out of trouble. Another role, and one which the German Navy exercised with limited success at the start of the war, was the interdiction of supply routes.

Today, only the United States and the Soviet Union continue to build cruisers. Purpose-built for the air defence role and carrying powerful surface-to-air missile armament in place of guns, their task is to operate in high-threat areas as an integral and vital part of a naval task force.

The first American warship design to carry SAMs as its primary armament was the USS *Leahy*, which initially carried two twin Terrier Mk 10 launchers fore and aft, and later adopted the SM2-ER Standard missile system. The *Leahy* class was followed by

nine warships of the *Belknap* class, which were also initially armed with the Terrier anti-aircraft missile system. Two cruisers of this class, the USS *Sterret* and USS *Biddle*, saw action in the Vietnam War; on 19 April 1972, the *Sterret* used one of her Terriers to destroy a North Vietnamese Styx anti-ship Cruise missile (the first time such an engagement took place in combat) and also two MiG-17s, one at a range of 17 miles. On 19 July, the USS *Biddle*'s Terriers shot down two more MiGs at a range of 20 miles.

### THE WESTERN WAY
Fifteen cruisers of the USS *Ticonderoga* class are equipped with the highly sophisticated Aegis weapon system. Based on the existing SM2-ER Standard missile, this is intended to offer US Navy battle groups protection against co-ordinated saturation attacks by anti-ship cruise missiles. The

*The USS* Leahy *was followed by eight more warships of her class, all built between 1962 and 1964. They have now been extensively modified.*

*HMS* Manchester *is one of the latest Type 42 destroyers. Her sister ships are HMS* Gloucester, *HMS* York *and HMS* Edinburgh.

system received some criticism in the summer of 1988, when the Aegis-equipped USS *Vincennes* shot down an Iranian Airbus which had been mistaken for an attacking warplane, but it was later established that the data supplied by the system had been misinterpreted through human error. The *Vincennes* was under threat from Iranian attack craft at the time, and the crew workload was high.

The Royal Navy's 'goalkeepers' are the Type 42 destroyers and Type 22 frigates, the former equipped with the long-range British Aerospace Sea Dart and the latter with the close-range Sea Wolf. Both weapons were used effectively in the Falklands conflict, and on 25 February 1991, in the final stage of the Gulf War, two Sea Darts launched from the destroyer HMS *Gloucester* destroyed an Iraqi Silkworm missile heading for the battleship USS *Missouri*. Two Silkworms were in fact fired; a Sea Dart scored a direct hit on the first and the second ditched in the sea shortly after being launched.

## THE EASTERN WAY

The Soviet Navy's battle groups have recently upgraded their anti-aircraft capability with the introduction of three new short-range SA missile systems, the SA-N-9, SA-N-10 and SA-N-11. These are deployed on numerous vessels, including the cruisers *Kirov, Frunze* and *Kalinin,* the *Kiev*-class aircraft carrier *Baku,* and the new attack carriers *Tbilisi* and *Riga.* The SA-N-11 is a new point-defence

*The* Novorossiysk *was the third of four warships in the Kiev-class of V/STOL aircraft and helicopter carriers. The others are the* Minsk *and* Baku.

missile, eight being tube-mounted on an advanced cannon/missile/fire-control radar close-in weapon system (CIWS). This features two 30 mm Gatling-type rotary cannon as well as the missiles, and is designed to saturate close-range aircraft and missile threats.

The Soviet Navy's policy is to equip all vessels in a battle group with a formidable air defence capability, rather than rely on purpose-built 'goalkeepers'.

Some warships have no fewer than four different SAM systems, starting with the SA-N-4 ; this can engage targets, including sea-skimming Cruise missiles, from sea level up to nearly 100,000 ft at a range of up to 62 miles. The SA-N-4 operates in conjunction with the 'Top Dome' fire control radar system.

# DESTROYING THE AIR THREAT   SAMs for now and tomorrow

**P**RESENT-DAY naval surface-to-air missiles trace their origins back to 1944, when the United States launched a crash programme to develop such weapons in response to Japanese *Kamikaze* suicide attacks on US naval task forces in the Pacific. Testing of the first naval SAM, called Little Joe, was well under way by February 1945, but the programme was abandoned because of ongoing development problems. The name Bumblebee was given to the

research and development programme, which also led to the design of another SAM called Lark and, eventually, to operational area-defence systems such as Talos, Terrier, Tartar, and the Standard Missile which is still a first-line naval defence system today.

Today's warships fight with all the available modern technology of radar and computers, all directing a few missile launchers, but they are more deadly than the myriad guns of yesteryear.

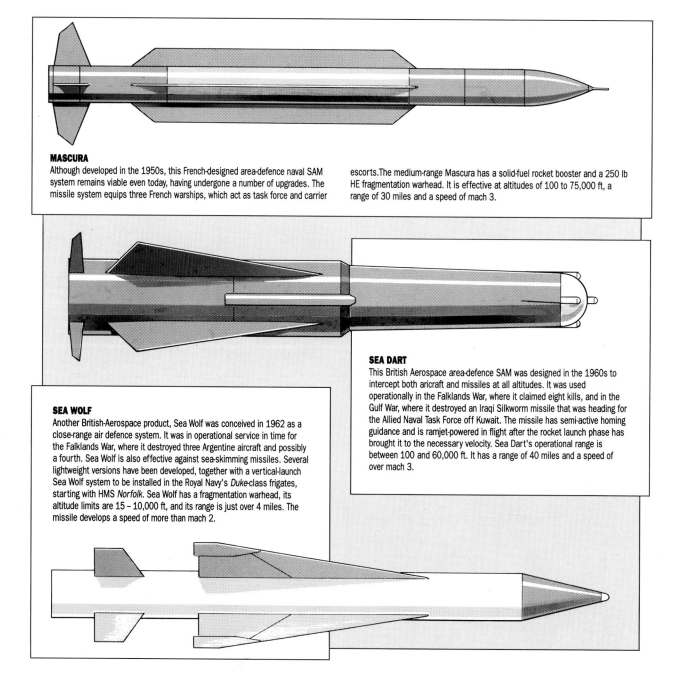

**MASCURA**
Although developed in the 1950s, this French-designed area-defence naval SAM system remains viable even today, having undergone a number of upgrades. The missile system equips three French warships, which act as task force and carrier escorts.The medium-range Mascura has a solid-fuel rocket booster and a 250 lb HE fragmentation warhead. It is effective at altitudes of 100 to 75,000 ft, a range of 30 miles and a speed of mach 3.

**SEA DART**
This British Aerospace area-defence SAM was designed in the 1960s to intercept both aricraft and missiles at all altitudes. It was used operationally in the Falklands War, where it claimed eight kills, and in the Gulf War, where it destroyed an Iraqi Silkworm missile that was heading for the Allied Naval Task Force off Kuwait. The missile has semi-active homing guidance and is ramjet-powered in flight after the rocket launch phase has brought it to the necessary velocity. Sea Dart's operational range is between 100 and 60,000 ft. It has a range of 40 miles and a speed of over mach 3.

**SEA WOLF**
Another British-Aerospace product, Sea Wolf was conceived in 1962 as a close-range air defence system. It was in operational service in time for the Falklands War, where it destroyed three Argentine aircraft and possibly a fourth. Sea Wolf is also effective against sea-skimming missiles. Several lightweight versions have been developed, together with a vertical-launch Sea Wolf system to be installed in the Royal Navy's *Duke*-class frigates, starting with HMS *Norfolk*. Sea Wolf has a fragmentation warhead, its altitude limits are 15 – 10,000 ft, and its range is just over 4 miles. The missile develops a speed of more than mach 2.

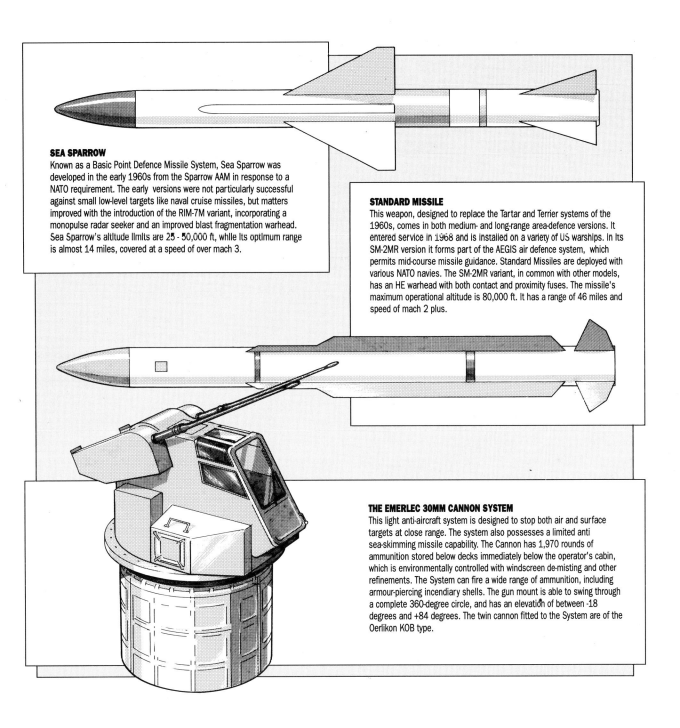

### SEA SPARROW

Known as a Basic Point Defence Missile System, Sea Sparrow was developed in the early 1960s from the Sparrow AAM in response to a NATO requirement. The early versions were not particularly successful against small low-level targets like naval cruise missiles, but matters improved with the introduction of the RIM-7M variant, incorporating a monopulse radar seeker and an improved blast fragmentation warhead. Sea Sparrow's altitude limits are 25 - 50,000 ft, while its optimum range is almost 14 miles, covered at a speed of over mach 3.

### STANDARD MISSILE

This weapon, designed to replace the Tartar and Terrier systems of the 1960s, comes in both medium- and long-range area-defence versions. It entered service in 1968 and is installed on a variety of US warships. In its SM-2MR version it forms part of the AEGIS air defence system, which permits mid-course missile guidance. Standard Missiles are deployed with various NATO navies. The SM-2MR variant, in common with other models, has an HE warhead with both contact and proximity fuses. The missile's maximum operational altitude is 80,000 ft. It has a range of 46 miles and speed of mach 2 plus.

### THE EMERLEC 30MM CANNON SYSTEM

This light anti-aircraft system is designed to stop both air and surface targets at close range. The system also possesses a limited anti sea-skimming missile capability. The Cannon has 1,970 rounds of ammunition stored below decks immediately below the operator's cabin, which is environmentally controlled with windscreen de-misting and other refinements. The System can fire a wide range of ammunition, including armour-piercing incendiary shells. The gun mount is able to swing through a complete 360-degree circle, and has an elevation of between -18 degrees and +84 degrees. The twin cannon fitted to the System are of the Oerlikon KOB type.

### NAVAL LASER WEAPON

Laser dazzle sights, designed to confuse and dazzle pilots of attacking aircraft, already form part of naval defence systems. They have been in service with the Royal Navy since the early 1980s, the policy being to fit them to any ship entering a potential danger zone. British Type 22 frigates normally carry two LDS. These sights were developed from industrial lasers and have an effective range of about three miles. With development, defensive laser weapons are likely to form an important aspect of naval defensive weaponry in the future.

CLASSIFIED

# CHAPTER THIRTEEN

# RUN SILENT, RUN DEEP

**T**HE *concept of submarine warfare is by no means a product of the 20th century. In 1634, two French priests, Fathers Mersenne and Fornier, produced quite a detailed design for an armed underwater craft, and in 1648 John Wilkins, who was Oliver Cromwell's brother-in-law, discussed the possibilities of a 'Submarine Ark'.*

*The first really practical submarine, and the first in the world to be mechanically powered when submerged, was the* Resurgam *(meaning 'I shall arise') of 1879. She was the brainchild of an English inventor, the Reverend George Garrett of Moss Side, Manchester.*

*By the outbreak of the First World War, in 1914, the submarine was well established in all the major navies of the world. In 1917 the threat from German U-Boats to British commerce was dire, and in April that year they sank 893,000 tons of shipping, of which 555,110 tons were British vessels.*

*The British developed countermeasures. They attacked and neutralized the main U-Boat bases on the Channel coast at Ostend and Zeebrugge, and built the so-called Dover Barrage, consisting of heavily-armed ships moored in lines across the Channel with minefields, nets and other obstacles between them. The barrage was a success, and between 1 January and 18 August 1918, 30 German submarines were destroyed as they tried to pass it.*

*The early successes of the German Navy's U-Boat arm were not forgotten by Nazi Germany's naval planners. The ocean-going U-Boat was to be a fearsome weapon in the Second World War, and one that came close to bringing Britain to her knees in the bitter conflict known as the Battle of the Atlantic.*

*Despite the technical excellence of their boats and the skill and courage of their crews, the Germans lost that battle because the Allies, in*

North Atlantic 1943: a German U-Boat sinks under the fierce onslaught of an RAF Coastal Commands Liberator's depth charges and guns.

*particular the British, brought air and sea co-operation to a fine art in the hunt for the sub-marines.*

*Long-range maritime patrol aircraft, equipped with new detection radar, enjoyed increasing success in locating and destroying the U-Boats.*

*The same aircraft co-operated on a magnificent scale with Royal Navy and US Navy 'hunter-killer' groups, composed of fast destroyers that combed the ocean for submarines in a highly-organized pattern and hounded them to destruction.*

*The final cost to the German Navy's U-Boat Service was appalling. Of the 1,162 U-Boats built and commissioned during the war, 785 were recorded as* spurlos versenkt - *a term that sounds even more chilling in German than its English equivalent, 'lost without trace'.*

*Of the 40,000 officers and men who served in U-*

Boats from 1939 to 1945, 30,000 never returned. Yet there was no escaping the fact that the U-Boats, in those years of war, had sunk 2,828 Allied merchant ships totalling 14,687,231 tons.

The lesson was well absorbed by the Soviet Navy, who in the early years of the Cold War set about building the largest submarine fleet in the world, its new craft incorporating much captured German design expertise.

By the late 1950s, the submarine was seen as an instrument that could decide the outcome of a war - perhaps even a non-nuclear war - fought on the high seas.

The United States could not match the USSR in terms of submarine production, but it could outstrip it technologically. In 1954, the US Navy, commissioned its first nuclear-powered submarine, the USS Nautilus, and within three years was experimenting with submarine-launched ballistic missiles.

The first of these, the Polaris A-1, achieved a limited operational capability in 1960, and in 1962 was replaced by the more potent Polaris A-2. The Russians quickly developed their own first-generation combination of nuclear-powered submarine and medium-range missiles, and although they never quite succeeded in catching up with the Americans in terms of equipment performance, they now had an additional means of delivering a devastating first strike against the continental United States.

So it was that the ballistic missile nuclear submarine (SSBN) became the super-powers' new capital ship, hiding in the remote ocean depths under the Arctic ice-cap, pitting its computerized wits against those of the forces that hunted it.

Despite the ever-changing political world scene, this is one deadly game of cat and mouse that still goes on.

The Royal Navy's *Resolution*-class SSBNs carry 16 Polaris A3TK ballistic missiles each. These have three 60 kt MIRV warheads

# THE REAL - LIFE HUNT FOR 'RED OCTOBER'

## A duel of wits for supremacy under the sea

THE most effective single weapon system for detecting and attacking enemy submarines is another submarine, the hunter-killer.

These fast, quiet, nuclear-powered craft hunt their quarry by listening with sensitive sonar devices based on large hydrophones mounted on the hull. The most advanced of these sensors use light-weight plastic sheets fastened to the hull. These generate electric impulses in response to minute acoustic pressure waves. The resulting signals are processed by a computer.

Using a technique called adaptive sensing, the computer selects the most promising frequency bands and automatically adjusts the sonar to listen more sharply. Once within range, the attack submarine can kill its enemy with an acoustic homing torpedo, which uses its own sonar to guide it in for a hit.

Apart from its high-tech sensory systems, the main advantage of the hunter-killer submarine is that it can remain submerged on patrol for virtually unlimited periods. Its diving depth can match, and often exceed, that of the most modern ballistic-missile armed submarines (SSBNs), and it has a very high speed underwater - so high, in fact, that it is capable of out-running torpedoes that might be fired against it.

### CHANGING PATHS OF DEVELOPMENT

The USA and USSR both began developing hunter-killer attack submarines in the late 1940s, but the development paths diverged over the years. The Americans concentrated on boats armed with torpedo-tube launched weapons, these craft being designated as SSNs. The Russians developed submarines capable of launching both torpedoes and anti-ship missiles. Such submarines carry the designation SSGN.

Modern nuclear submarines are designed to be very quiet. When cruising on patrol at low speed, a submarine may radiate only 0.01 watt of acoustic power, less than the noise of a car passing along a highway. Soviet nuclear submarines, although much improved over the past few years, have always been noisier than their American counterparts, especially at high speed. Even a noisy submarine radiates less than one watt, but the sound can be picked up at incredibly long distances.

'The first time the Soviets put the pedal to the metal on an Alpha-class *boat*,' declared one American anti-submarine warfare (ASW) specialist, '*the noise travelled all the way to Bermuda.*' The Russian submarine was in the Barents Sea at the time, 4,000 miles away.

### THE FASTEST SUBMARINE IN THE WORLD

The *Alpha*-class submarine is the world's fastest and deepest-diving SSN. It is constructed from titanium alloy and uses an advanced nuclear reactor with a liquid metal coolant, a system rejected by the Americans as being too complex for installation in a submarine.

*Alpha* has an operational diving depth of 2,297 ft, and can go down to a maximum of 3,805 ft in an emergency. One major advantage of the titanium hull is that it reduces the submarine's magnetic anomaly signature, making the boat very hard to detect during its underwater passage.

Magnetic anomaly detectors rely on picking up 'kinks' in the Earth's magnetic field caused by the passage of a large iron-bearing object, but the only ferrous metal in an *Alpha* boat is inside the hull itself. *Alpha*'s hull is also coated with a material called 'Clusterguard', which gives it a stealth capability in that it reduces the efficiency of active sonar transmissions.

*Alpha* has six torpedo tubes and carries a normal operational armament of eight 21 in anti-ship torpedoes, ten 16 in anti-submarine torpedoes, two anti-ship or anti-submarine nuclear torpedoes and two SS-N-15 anti-submarine nuclear missiles. Both nuclear weapons have a warhead yield of 15 kilotons. The submarine, which has a crew of 45, has an underwater speed of 45 knots.

*Alpha* is a third-generation Soviet SSN; the first was the *November*-class, the prototype of which was launched in 1963. *November* was rushed into service before its reactor system was perfected, and there were many instances of radiation-related illnesses among its crews. It was followed into service by the much more effective *Victor*-class SSN, a series that has been steadily improved since the first *Victor* I entered service in the late 1960s. Two more Soviet

*The Victor III is one of the quietest Russian nuclear submarines and is in service with both the Northern and Pacific Fleets.*

*Soviet* Akula-*class submarines have steel hulls. Note the towed sonar array pod positioned over the stern of the submarine.*

SSN classes, *Sierra* and *Akula*, are in service; the latter, launched in July 1984, a development of the *Victor* III. These later classes of submarine all have a towed sonar array in a pod on top of the upper rudder.

The US Navy's first SSN was the *Skipjack* class, which, built in the late 1950s, remained the USA's fastest submarine for 30 years. The first American SSN with advanced sonar equipment and deep-diving capability was the *Thresher* class, which could dive to a maximum depth of 1,970 ft. These boats were later renamed *Permit* class after the prototype, the USS *Thresher*, was lost with all 129 crew during its diving trials off the New England coast in April 1963.

**A NEW SUB WITH NEW WEAPONRY**
The *Permit* class of SSN introduced the SUBROC anti-submarine missile. Essentially a nuclear depth charge propelled by a solid-fuel rocket motor, SUBROC follows a short underwater course after launch from a submarine's torpedo tube, before transferring to an air trajectory for the major portion of its journey to the target. At a pre-determined point, the depth charge separates from the rocket booster and follows a ballistic trajectory to enter the water close to the target, after which it sinks to a pre-set depth and detonates. SUBROC reaches a speed of Mach 1.5 and has a maximum range of 35 miles; its five-kiloton W55 fission warhead has a lethal range against submarines of 3-4 miles from its detonation point.

SUBROC is considered to be a theatre tactical nuclear weapon, and clearance from the President of the United States would have to be obtained before it could be used.

It is carried aboard later class American SSNs like the USS *Sturgeon*, USS *Narwhal* and USS *Glenard P*

*Lipscomb*. It will be replaced in the 1990s by Sea Lance, a long-range ASW missile with a range of up to 100 miles.

## ON THE OTHER SIDE OF THE POND

The Royal Navy has an important hunter-killer role to play within NATO, and British SSN crews are acknowledged as being tactically very skilled in this type of operation. British SSN classes are HMS *Valiant*, HMS *Churchill*, HMS *Swiftsure* and HMS *Trafalgar*. Eighteen submarines in these classes are either in service or under construction.

The *Trafalgar*-class boats feature a number of improvements to reduce underwater noise, including a hull coating similar to the Russian 'Clusterguard' and a pump-jet propulsion system that does away with the need for a conventional propeller. The submarines carry an operational load of 20 Tigerfish torpedoes plus five Sub-Harpoon anti-ship missiles. Alternativly, 50 Stonefish or Sea Urchin mines can be

*HMS* Turbulant *is a* Trafalgar-*class nuclear attack submarine in service with the Royal Navy. A total of seven submarines of this class are due to be built with a further development on the drawing-board.*

stowed. As well as providing an ASW screen to protect Allied task forces, minelaying on the exit routes from enemy submarine bases would form a considerable part of the hunter-killer's task in time of war.

The smallest nuclear attack submarine in service with any navy is the French *Rubis* class. Five of these boats are in service with another five planned; these, forming two squadrons, will be based in Brest and Toulon, providing a defensive shield for the French SSBN fleet.

The French *Rubis*-class submarines carry an underwater-launched version of the Exocet anti-ship missile as well as torpedoes. They have a maximum diving depth of 1,640 ft and a submerged speed of 25 knots.

Diesel-powered submarines still have an important role to play in offensive underwater operations. Only the wealthier nations can afford to produce nuclear powerplants and their associated equipment. Diesel submarines have nowhere near the range and endurance of their bigger counterparts, but they are very quiet and, when operating in the 'silent running' state, are very hard to detect. One such Argentinian craft presented a constant threat to the British Task Force in the Falkland Islands.

# TORPEDOES AND MINES Tinfish...and Stonefish of the future

**D**URING the Second World War, and for some years afterwards, the torpedo was viewed essentially as an anti-surface vessel weapon. Then submarines had to operate close to the surface in order to use their schnorchel equipment, and because of their relatively slow submerged speed they often had to surface to set up a suitable attack pattern. They were therefore vulnerable to attack by depth charges, anti-submarine rockets and mortars; occasions on which torpedoes were used to sink submarines were extremely rare.

The advent of the nuclear-powered submarine (SSN) changed the pattern completely. Freed from the surface environment, the SSN is extremely difficult to detect, classify, locate and attack, especially with short-range systems such as depth charges and anti-submarine mortars. As a result, the torpedo has become the most flexible and effective anti-submarine weapon.

## STING RAY AND TIGERFISH

Great Britain, without doubt, leads the world in torpedo technology. The Sting Ray lightweight anti-submarine torpedo, for example, developed by Marconi Underwater Systems Ltd, is the most advanced of its kind in the world, and is claimed to be at least a generation ahead of any similar weapon system. It can be operated from a wide range of helicopters, fixed wing aircraft and surface ships. Once launched, Sting Ray seeks out submarine targets automatically; its computer sets up an appropriate attack pattern, analyses and rejects decoys and countermeasures, and computes the required track to guide the weapon to its target. It then attacks the target's most vulnerable area, using target data stored in the computer's memory.

The first launch of Sting Ray with a live warhead took place on 19 October 1985, the weapon being air-dropped from a Nimrod aircraft of No 42 (Torpedo Bomber) Squadron. Three minutes after entering the water, the torpedo impacted on the target submarine *Porpoise*, moored at a depth of 213 ft. Sting Ray's operational details are classified, but it is thought to be effective at depths of up to 3, 000 ft, matching the diving depths of the very latest

*The destructive power of a Mk 24 Tigerfish torpedo is self evident from this trials' photograph. Further explosions will break the ship's back.*

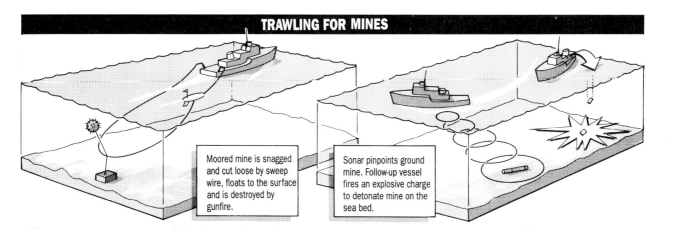

**TRAWLING FOR MINES**

Moored mine is snagged and cut loose by sweep wire, floats to the surface and is destroyed by gunfire.

Sonar pinpoints ground mine. Follow-up vessel fires an explosive charge to detonate mine on the sea bed.

Soviet nuclear submarines such as the *Typhoon* and *Akula*-class.

The Royal Navy's standard submarine-launched heavyweight torpedo is Tigerfish, which is guided from the firing submarines fire control equipment through a wire link. Once the torpedo's sonar has made contact with the target, its homing system takes over, carrying out the succeeding phases of the attack automatically. Like Sting Ray, Tigerfish can repeat its attack if initial contact is lost. The quietest long-range torpedo in the world, Tigerfish was the weapon that sank the Argentine cruiser *General Belgrano* in the Falklands War.

Eventually, Tigerfish will be replaced by another Marconi-developed heavyweight torpedo, Spearfish. Drawing on Sting Ray technology, Spearfish is extremely fast and very manoeuvrable. It is propelled by gas turbine, is wire guided and has an advanced acoustic homing system. Its powerful computers enable it to remain effective against the most modern countermeasures. It is claimed that Spearfish, although primarily an anti-submarine weapon, is capable of sinking warships of 40,000 tons (such as the Soviet *Kiev*-class aircraft carriers) with a single round, and that a salvo of two will sink any target.

In the arsenal of the world's navies, after the torpedo, the next most effective anti-submarine weapon is the mine.

**A FAMILY CALLED STONEFISH**

A mine's main function, when effectively deployed, is to act as a deterrent, restricting the operations of submarines and surface vessels. The modern mine is an intelligent, self-contained weapon system. Marconi's Stonefish family of ground mines - those that lie on the sea bed - provides a good example. Stonefish comes in four versions; two are used for training and exercise. The operational weapons are

the Stonefish Warstock Mine and the Stonefish Assessment Mine.

The Stonefish Warstock Mine can be launched from surface vessels, submarines and aircraft, different sizes of warhead being fitted according to the water depth and the selected minefield pattern. The Stonefish Assessment Mine is used for intelligence gathering; laid on the bottom of shipping channels and connected to a shore station, the mine is activated by passing shipping and sends data on a vessel's signature to the shore station, where it is processed and used to update target characteristics.

The mine can be either ship-launched or, as is often the case, dropped by parachute from a helicopter or aircraft.

The Soviet Union, however, is still the leading exponent of sea mine warfare, with over 400,000 of them on its naval weapons inventory.

*A Lynx helicopter launches a parachute-retarded Sting Ray torpedo.*

# SPECIAL OPS, SPECIAL MISSIONS
## When Whiskey and water don't mix

**O**VER the years, the submarine has proved to be a useful vehicle for all kinds of special operations. In the Second World War, submarines were used extensively by the Allies to deliver supplies and ammunition to beleaguered garrisons, to land commando teams and agents on enemy soil, and, in the Pacific, to liaise with 'coast watchers', agents positioned on Japanese-held islands to monitor the movements of enemy shipping.

In the latter weeks of the war in Europe, the Germans also used ocean-going U-Boats for a different kind of special mission: the secret transfer, to sympathetic Latin American countries, of top-ranking Nazis, who were on the Allies' 'Wanted' list.

### UNDERNEATH AND UNDERCOVER

The infiltration of special forces' combat teams is still one of the submarine's main clandestine functions. Such techniques are practised regularly by the US Navy's SEAL (Sea, Air and Land) commandos, men of the Royal Marines' Special Boat Squadron, and Soviet *Spetsnaz* (Special Assignment Force) troops. Some Russian *Whiskey*-class diesel-electric submarines were fitted with a deck-mounted diving chamber for use by *Spetsnaz* combat swimmers, such boats being widely used in the Baltic to probe the defences of Norway and Sweden.

These operations became public knowledge in the summer of 1980, when Swedish patrol aircraft tracked a Soviet submarine deep inside Sweden's territorial waters. The Swedes launched a three-week operation involving troops, aircraft, warships and the expenditure of dozens of depth charges in an effort to trap the elusive submarine, and much to their embarrassment failed to do so.

In the following year, however, it was the Russians' turn to be embarrassed when one of their *Whiskey*-class boats ran aground between the islands of Malkvarn and Torumskar, right in the middle of a heavily-defended Swedish military zone. The Russians lamely explained that the submarine's crew had made a navigational error because of compass failure, but the Swedes knew otherwise. The *Whiskey* boat was in their waters to probe a network of underwater obstacles and minefields which had recently been upgraded.

Intelligence-gathering operations by Soviet submarines, particularly off north-west Scotland and in the Western Approaches to the United Kingdom,

where Soviet boats lie in wait to monitor the passage of British and American ballistic missile submarines en route to and from the Upper Clyde, are thought to have been the cause of several accidents involving fishing vessels in recent years. Some admitted accidents were caused by Allied submarines in transit, but others remained a mystery.

## DISAPPEARING BOATS

Recent cases have included one in 1983, in which five crewmen died when the *Oite d'Aleth* disappeared off Wexford, Eire, and a companion trawler, the *Amie de Moulles*, was snagged and towed for some distance. In 1984, an unnamed trawler was towed five miles by a submarine that snagged its nets off Dublin. That same year the trawler *South Stack* disappeared, with the loss of three lives. Two other trawlers, the *Jean de Lorraine* and the *Joanne C* , were snagged by unidentified submarines. Later the *Jake II* vanished in a submarine exercise area.

In 1987, the trawler *Boy Shaun* disappeared in the Irish Sea, and an unidentified submarine was sighted in the area. The trawler *Summer Morn* was towed backwards for ten miles, and the *Port Logan* sank after striking a 'steel object' near the Isle of Man.

1988 saw the fishing vessel *Alliance* involved in a near collision with a submarine off the coast of Northern Ireland. The *Pearl* vanished in a submarine exercise area off Holyhead, and the *Dawn Waters* struck an underwater obstacle and sank in full view of other fishing craft.

In 1989 the *Tarrandale* disappeared, again in a submarine exercise area. Five crew died when the Belgian trawler *Tijl Ulenspiegel* vanished in the Irish Sea. Two more trawlers, the *Inspire* and *Girl Fiona*, also sank in mysterious circumstances.

In the past ten years, seventeen British and foreign fishing craft have disappeared as a result of submarine collisions, only a few of them involving USN and RN vessels. Many of the others were doubtless victims of the clandestine submarine war, an ongoing conflict in which the major navies of the world still regard one another through covert eyes.

*Spyships are designated AGIs (Intelligence Gathering Auxiliaries) in naval terms. This one, typical of those seen in northern waters, is a Okean-class converted trawler.*

# CHAPTER FOURTEEN

# FIND, FIX AND STRIKE

**A**T the outset of the Second World War, all flotilla vessels of the Royal Navy were fitted with the acoustic detection device called 'Asdic', which took its name from the initials of the Allied Submarine Devices Investigation Committee. It was an enormous advance on the hydrophone listening gear that had been used during the First World War, and in the hands of the Royal Navy's skilled operators it produced excellent results in detecting submarines during the fleet exercises of the 1930s.

The fact that such exercises tended to be unrealistic was ignored by the Admiralty, who adopted the equally unrealistic attitude that Asdic had, at last, provided surface warships with the ultimate means of combating the submarine menace. The bitter and costly battle of the Atlantic would soon give the lie to that theory.

The fact remains that sound was, and still is, the single most important factor in anti-submarine warfare. In the early years of the Second World War, the lack of any means of detecting enemy submarines by underwater radar echoes severely curtailed the efficiency of maritime patrol aircraft; a submarine had to be at least partially surfaced before air-to-surface vessel radar (ASV) could pick it up.

The first move towards rectifying this situation was made in February 1942, when the US National Defense Research Committee developed an expendable sonobuoy for use by lighter-than-air craft (airships) in anti-submarine warfare (ASW). On 7 March, the idea was demonstrated in an exercise off New London, Connecticut, when the US Navy's Goodyear non-rigid airship, the K-5, working in conjunction with the submarine S20, dropped a series of test sonobuoys.

It was found that the buoy could detect the sound of the submerged submarine's propellers at a distance of up to three miles, while radio reception of the buoy's signals aboard the 'blimp'

was satisfactory up to five miles away.

In October, the C-in-C US Fleet directed the Bureau of Ships to procure 1,000 sonobuoys and 100 associated receivers, and this equipment became operational with Fleet Airship Group One at Lakehurst, New Jersey, early in 1943. By the end of the war, sonobuoys were widely used by all Allied airborne ASW forces.

Although the development of ASV radar began in the 1930s, as a natural progression of the work undertaken by Robert Watson-Watt and other scientists on early warning radar, it was not until late in 1940 that real strides were made in evaluating and refining ASV techniques. In December 1939, the first airborne radar detection of a submarine was made off Gosport, in southern England, at an unrecorded but very short range; and the first radar-assisted attack on a U-Boat was made by a Short Sunderland fitted with ASV Mk I, in November 1940. Then, in

---

An experimental ASV housing under the nose of a Handley Page Halifax, an aircraft type much used by the RAF for anti-submarine operations during the Second World War.

The Avro Shackleton - seen here in South African Air Force markings - was one of the world's leading maritime patrol aircraft in the 1950s.

February 1941, an Armstrong-Whitworth Whitley achieved the first radar-assisted U-Boat sinking with the aid of ASV Mk II.

By early 1943, ASV equipment was capable of detecting surfaced submarines at a range of 20 nautical miles, and the number of U-Boat sightings by aircraft increased dramatically. The effective range of the equipment grew with further development and the German Navy frantically sought countermeasures.

By mid-1944, just at a time when the Allied maritime air forces were putting their considerable radar potential to good tactical use, the German U-Boat service had the benefit of two major advances.

The first was the Type XXI U-Boat which, with a high underwater speed, large battery capacity and strengthened hull, was capable of long submerged transits and presented only a small radar target when on the surface. The second was the Schnorchel (or Snorkel) air inlet pipe which, when raised just above the surface, enabled the U-Boat to recharge its batteries while remaining submerged.

The most effective ASV set in service at the end of the war was the Mk XIII, which was installed in the Avro Shackleton maritime patrol aircraft in the 1950s. The last Shackleton maritime patrol variant, the Mk 3, was equipped with the ASV Mk XXI, and this was inherited by its successor, the Nimrod MR 1.

In the 1950s the RAF also used the Lockheed P2V Neptune for maritime patrol work. This was also the US Navy's primary type, tasked with the same mission until it was replaced by the P-3 Orion, an aircraft that also serves with a number of foreign naval air arms.

The French Navy uses the Breguet Atlantic, as does the German Marineflieger. The Atlantic is powered by two Rolls-Royce Tyne turboprop engines.

In recent years, advances in airborne submarine detection equipment have greatly enhanced the effectiveness of the maritime patrol aircraft. Yet the fact is that the submarine still remains one step ahead of its hunters.

# PASSING CLOUDS   When the sky rules the waves

**R**ECONNAISSANCE satellites today play a vital role in tracking the movements of potentially hostile submarines. Since satellite equipment does not yet have the ability to peer into the ocean depths, reconnaissance involves constant surveillance of submarine bases and electronic data gathering by monitoring submarine radar and communications transmissions.

One of the most highly classified surveillance systems is the US Whitecloud series of satellites, the first of which was placed in orbit on 30 April 1976. Developed for the US Naval Research Laboratory by Martin Marietta, Whitecloud are injected into a 700-mile-high orbit, where they release three smaller spacecraft that fan out to cover a wider area. The project was so secret that Naval Research Laboratory personnel were not even allowed to use the word Whitecloud in telephone conversations, until, that is, it suddenly appeared on souvenir postal covers at the tourist gift shop in the cafeteria at NASA's Johnson Space Center, in October 1984!

### BLACK MISSIONS

All American ocean surveillance satellite systems come under the 'Deep Black' (Highly Secret) security classification. They include the Big Bird and the later Key Hole (KH-11/12) series of photographic reconnaissance satellites, which provide round-the-clock coverage of Soviet and Chinese submarine bases.

Designed by Lockheed and known officially as Broad Coverage Photo Reconnaissance Satellites (Code 467), the Big Bird series has been operational since 1971. These satellites orbit at between 100 and 150 miles and have a useful life of about six months, so replacing them is an ongoing process. As well as taking photographs with high-resolution optical cameras. Big Bird is equipped to conduct both television and radio surveillance. Film capsules are ejected from the parent satellite and are recovered in mid-air as they descend under a parachute.

Key Hole satellites, described elsewhere in this book, transmit photographic data to ground stations in digitized form.

It may soon be possible for satellites to detect submarines under water with the aid of 'blue-green' laser systems. These are now under development by the US Navy and the Defense Advanced Research Projects Agency (DARPA) as part of a programme

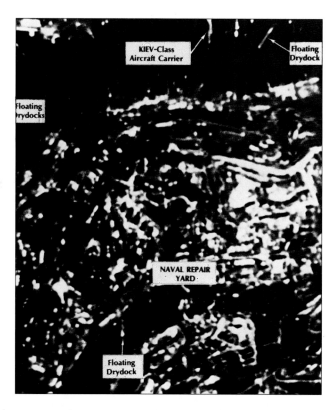

*The important naval base of Vladivostok, headquarters of the Soviet Pacific Fleet is kept under regular satellite surveillance.*

designed to improve communications with submerged submarines.

Water may not look like a barrier to communications, but appearances are deceptive. Water strongly absorbs all electromagnetic waves except blue-green light and extremely low frequency (ELF) radio waves. The very low frequency (VLF) waves used for many years to contact submarines penetrate only a short distance into the ocean, so the craft must either surface or send up antennas to receive messages, thereby increasing its vulnerability. A laser system, accurate over long distances and capable of carrying more data than VLF waves, would communicate with submarines at their normal cruising depths and so be able drastically to reduce the chance of detection.

Two blue-green laser systems are being considered. In one, a laser based on the ground or in an aircraft is beamed to a mirror-carrying satellite in a 22,500-mile orbit; the mirror reflects and guides

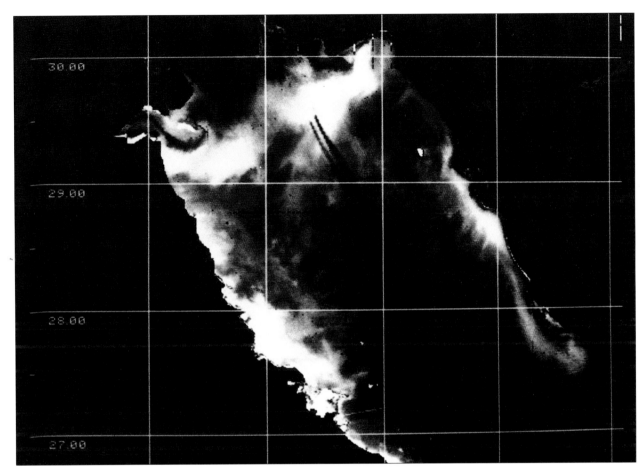

*This view of the Gulf, taken by a Nimbus Weather satellite, shows pollution from shattered Kuwaiti oil installations.*

the light to the vicinity of the submarine. In the other, a message is radioed to a satellite-borne laser, converted to light signals and beamed down to the ocean. Messages would be encoded as a series of short, powerful pulses of laser light no brighter than a medium star.

**MAKING BEAMS 'ECO' SAFE**

In both systems, a very diffuse, broad beam would be scanned over thousands of square miles of ocean so that it would not endanger boats, birds or fish - nor the submarines it has to reach. Military planners are concerned that a narrow light beam, scattered by atmospheric dust or reflected by the ocean, could help enemy satellites pinpoint the receiving submarines.

Since only a small fraction of the laser beam will make its way through the air and ocean, receivers mounted on the submarines must be able not only to detect the laser but to discriminate between it and sunlight. Military scientists are now working on special filters that allow through only the precise wavelengths emitted by the laser. The filtered light, when transformed into electrical signals, can then be decoded.

Although the laser concept is promising, ELF communications systems are already in limited operational use. The drawback is that such systems require lengthy transmitting antennas.

The first ELF prototype, built in 1969, used an overhead antenna that was no less than 28 miles long, and an operational version uses an antenna that is three times as long, taking an unacceptably large area of ground. The US Navy also uses aircraft fitted with trailing aerials to communicate with submarines in times of emergency, under a system called TACAMO (Take Charge and Move Out).

# THE SILENT LISTENERS Looking for sound signatures in the ocean

FOR a long time, one of the principal systems used to detect Soviet submarines by NATO's ASW forces has been SOSUS (Sound Surveillance System), a permanent array of hydrophones positioned in the sea bed at intervals on a track running roughly between Norway's North Cape via Iceland to Newfoundland.

SOSUS listens for the sound signatures of passing submarines and transmits them to a signal processing computer onshore. The computer asks its memory whether the signals have the frequencies of the propeller and machinery noises one would expect from a particular class of submarine. It also introduces time delays into the hydrophone signals, to represent the time it would take sound from the submarine's possible location to reach each hydrophone. The system does not pinpoint submarines, but it can determine their position in a circle with a radius of less than 50 miles, well within the detection capability of modern ASW aircraft. From then on, fixing the submarine's exact position becomes a job for ASW's most widely used underwater detection system - the sonobuoy.

## DUNKING OR DIPPING BUOYS

Modern sonobuoys vary in length from 1 ft to about 4 ft. The smaller versions, which weigh around 10 lb, can be dropped from any altitude from 40,000 ft down to 150 ft at airspeeds between 50 knots and 350 knots. These criteria are set by the time required to deploy a drogue parachute or ballonet for stabilization. The latter is important, as the sonobuoy must enter the water cleanly to ensure that the impact shock is absorbed by the correct portion of the buoy. Equally important is the need to avoid a series of splashes as the hydrophone leads unreel to their operating depth. The sound, magnified underwater, can alert a submarine commander to the presence of the detection device.

When the sonobuoy enters the sea, the drogue parachute is released and water enters the housing to activate a sea-water battery. A carbon dioxide ($CO_2$) cylinder is then fired to inflate a float bag with an integral antenna. At the same time the descent housing, which protects the hydrophone head, detaches from the main body and sinks to a preselected depth, at which point it separates from the

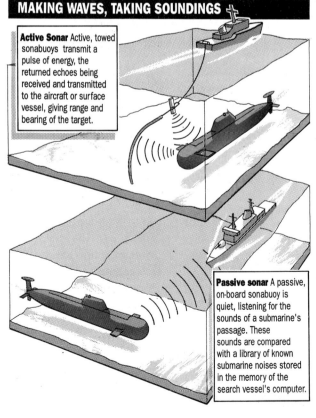

**MAKING WAVES, TAKING SOUNDINGS**

**Active Sonar** Active, towed sonabuoys transmit a pulse of energy, the returned echoes being received and transmitted to the aircraft or surface vessel, giving range and bearing of the target.

**Passive sonar** A passive, on-board sonabuoy is quiet, listening for the sounds of a submarine's passage. These sounds are compared with a library of known submarine noises stored in the memory of the search vessel's computer.

transducer and the buoy becomes operational. The hydrophone depth can be selected between 60 and 1,000 ft.

The datalink between the buoy and the aircraft is on a pre-selected channel in the very high frequency (VHF) spectrum. A sonobuoy's life in the water is pre-set before launch and is usually one, four or eight hours, at which point the buoy self-scuttles to avoid being picked up by enemy forces or becoming a hazard to shipping.

## HOW SALTY IS THE SEA?

As sea conditions can vary from day to day, the sonics operators require a direct readout of temperature and salinity against depth, to plot any heat layers which may either hide a target or interfere with the underwater path of sonic signals. This is achieved by dropping a device called a bathythermobuoy, which is similar in size and shape to a sonobuoy, and which deploys a sinker at the rate of 3 ft per second to take salinity and temperature readings from the surface down to about 1,000 ft.

The measurements are then transmitted back to the aircraft, where a three-dimensional plot of the undersea conditions can be constructed. Sonobuoys can then be positioned at locations covering various depths where conditions might be concealing a vessel.

Submarines generate two types of noise, discrete and broadband. Isolated noise is generated by machinery such as motors, pumps and propellors, while broadband noise is caused by the passage of the submarine through the water. Technology has greatly reduced the volume of discrete noise; however it can still be very noisy. But it can be identified by a skilled operator searching for characteristic frequencies, based on a computer library of sound 'signatures' applicable to individual submarine types painstakingly built up over the years by Naval Intelligence. This is the key to modern anti-submarine warfare.

*The Lockheed P-3 Orion. This very effective ASW aircraft equips several naval air arms all over the world.*

# DETECTION AND ATTACK FROM ON HIGH
## How helicopters meet the detection challenge

**A**LTHOUGH long-endurance maritime patrol aircraft like the British Aerospace Nimrod and the Lockheed P-3 Orion - with their ability to cover vast areas of ocean in a single sortie - are vital to ASW operations, the helicopter has become a primary anti-submarine weapon in protecting naval task forces.

Helicopter ASW operations have changed, since the 1970s, with the introduction of the newer, quieter classes of Soviet submarines which were far harder to detect than their predecessors. Speed became an ASW helicopter requirement, for once a contact had been picked up by the parent vessel's sonar, the helicopter had to be on the scene quickly to re-detect, classify, pinpoint, track and if necessary attack the suspect vessel.

The need for a small, fast, armed helicopter designed to operate from cruisers, destroyers and frigates was by no means new. The helicopter that filled the Royal Navy's requirement in this respect,

*Seen here demonstrating its dipping sonar technique for the camera, this Westland Sea King has the ability to spend half its mission time in this activity.*

from 1963, was the Westland Wasp, which operated from a platform mounted on the aft end of a frigate and which carried two Mk 44 homing torpedoes as its standard armament.

The American equivalent, which entered USN service at about the same time, was the Kaman SH-2 Seasprite. Neither helicopter carried its own detection equipment and remained under the control of the parent vessel at all times, which limited the area of sea that could be patrolled for submarines to a 20-mile radius, or an area of about 1,200 square miles.

### SIKORSKY'S NEW HELO
Today, Soviet submarines carry torpedoes with a range in excess of 50 miles, and anti-ship Cruise missiles with a much greater range. The sea area that must be swept for submarines has increased to a 100-mile radius - 30,000 square miles. To meet this new requirement, the small-ship helicopter must be armed with its own detection apparatus, so that it can operate independently of its parent vessel during the last phase of search and attack.

In April 1984, the first batch of Sikorsky SH-60 Seahawk anti-submarine helicopters were delivered to the US Navy. Developed from the UH-60 Blackhawk, the SH-60 is equipped with the Light Airborne Multipurpose System (LAMPS) Mk III mission system, comprising search radar, sonobuoy acoustic processor, towed magnetic anomaly detection (MAD) equipment, electronic support measures (ESM) and datalink. The helicopter and its sensors are controlled by the parent vessel until the Seahawk descends below the horizon to locate and attack independently. Armament includes Mk 46 torpedoes, air-to-surface missiles or depth bombs. A further version, the SH-60C, equipped with a Bendix AQS-13F dipping sonar, a Teledyne ASN-123 tactical navigation computer and armed with Mk 50 torpedoes, has been developed to provide 'inner zone' ASW defence, operating close to a task force.

### WESTLAND'S WAY OF DOING THINGS
A similar role is carried out by the Royal Navy's Westland Lynx, which replaced the Wasp as the RN's standard multi-role small-ship helicopter. Longer-range operations are carried out by the Westland Sea King HAS 5, which differs from its US Navy counterpart, the SH-3, in that it has the ability to

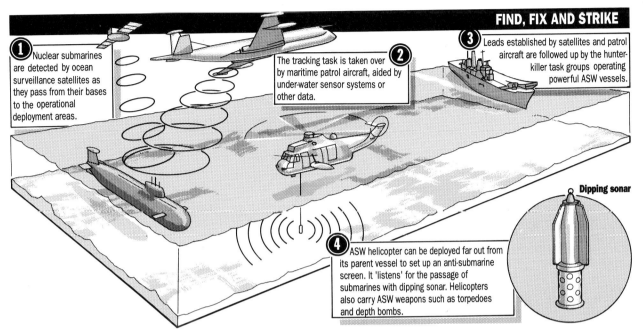

FIND, FIX AND STRIKE

**①** Nuclear submarines are detected by ocean surveillance satellites as they pass from their bases to the operational deployment areas.

The tracking task is taken over by maritime patrol aircraft, aided by under-water sensor systems or other data. **②**

**③** Leads established by satellites and patrol aircraft are followed up by the hunter-killer task groups operating powerful ASW vessels.

Dipping sonar

**④** ASW helicopter can be deployed far out from its parent vessel to set up an anti-submarine screen. It 'listens' for the passage of submarines with dipping sonar. Helicopters also carry ASW weapons such as torpedoes and depth bombs.

track and destroy enemy submarines without the assistance of the parent vessel.

The Sea King is equipped with Sea-Searcher radar and a version of the GEC-Marconi AQS-902, which combines acoustic processing for both sonobuoys and dipping sonar. The helicopter has a crew of five and an endurance of four hours, providing anti-submarine cover at a combat radius of up to 200 miles from its home base.

The Royal Navy's principal counter to the threat of the new generation of ultra-quiet Soviet submarines in the 1990s will be the navalized version of the European Helicopter Industries EH 101 helicopter, which will have twice the range and payload of the Sea King.

Because of its size, the EH 101 - which will be named Merlin in RN service - has the capacity to carry radar, electronic support measures, forward-looking infra-red, sonobuoys, dipping sonar and MAD equipment - in fact, the complete ASW package.

Radar is the primary sensor against surface targets, including submarine periscopes which can be detected even in high seas using a pulse-compression radar. Radars like this are normally fitted to large maritime patrol aircraft, but the Merlin will have the Ferrant Blue Kestrel, a new pulse-compression radar developed specifically for the helicopter.

*The US Navy's Seahawk, resplendent in a high-visibility camouflage. The first batch of these sophisticated ASW helicopters was handed over in 1984.*

# THE MIGHTY HUNTER OF THE OCEAN SKIES
## How Nimrod seeks its prey

I N the late 1970s, the Royal Air Force discovered that advances in Soviet submarine technology were beginning to outstrip the search and surveillance equipment installed in its British Aerospace Nimrod MR I maritime patrol aircraft, which equipped four squadrons of the RAF's No 18 (Maritime) Group, and formed a vital element of NATO's anti-submarine warfare resources. Developed from the de Havilland Comet 4 civil airliner, and powered by four Rolls-Royce Spey turbofan engines, the Nimrod had begun to replace the RAF's

*The British Aerospace Nimrod MR2, a key weapon in NATO's anti-submarine inventory, overflies one of her escort ships.*

ageing Shackletons in October 1969.

The RAF's answer to the new submarine threat was to develop the Nimrod MR 2. The airframe and engines remained basically the same, but the new variant was fitted with a range of ASW systems that gave it an operational capability far in advance of its predecessor's.

The Nimrod MR 2's Thorn EMC Searchwater ASV radar is the most advanced of its kind in the world. It is designed to detect and classify small targets against the high clutter (background interference) caused by heavy seas and bad weather, and in this respect it has about 50 times the performance of the ASV Mk XXI which the Nimrod MR I inherited from the Shackleton. The system is largely computer-controlled, which provides very high performance

while keeping the operator's workload down to a manageable level. If only one sector is of interest, the computer decides automatically whether to continue rotation of the radar antenna and illuminate a wider area, or whether only to scan backwards and forwards over that particular area. The computer also has a built-in system that keeps the false alarm rate down. IFF (Identification Friend or Foe) is also integrated into Searchwater, which has weather and navigation functions as well as search. Track-while-scan capability is extensive, but the number of targets which can be tracked individually is classified, as is the radar's range.

At the heart of the Nimrod Mk 2's effectiveness is the GEC Avionics AQS-901 acoustic processor. The aircraft carries two of these systems, each of which is able to receive data from up to eight sonobuoys. Processed information is presented on cathode-ray tube displays and hard copy recorders for analysis by the Nimrod's tactical commander. The system is also fitted with a Canadian-built computing device, the Fast Fourier Transform (FFT) analyser, which separates the frequencies that make up a received signal. This allows regular noise, that may be generated by a submarine's reactor, for example, to be amplified above the background of random noise caused by the ocean, even though the sea's sound might be much stronger at that moment.

**DETECT THEN SEARCH**

The Nimrod, like all other maritime patrol aircraft, uses three types of sonobuoy to detect, identify and pinpoint a submarine prior to carrying out an attack. The aircraft first of all sows a pattern of passive omni-directional buoys to provide overlapping coverage of an area where there is a suspected target. Once this has been confirmed, passive directional buoys are dropped to identify it, and it is then pinpointed at the last minute by active directional buoys.

The AD sonobuoy used by the Nimrod is the British-designed CAMBS, which provides sufficient data on target bearing, range and Doppler relative speed for the AQS 901 to track the submarine. CAMBS is a command-active buoy, which delays the submarine commander's awareness that he is under attack until the final stage. Having dropped its passive buoys, the Nimrod circles and then begins its attack-run along the submarine's anticipated

*Monitoring sonar transmissions, prior to ordering in a Nimrod to investigate .*

track, the run-in being made from the submarine's six o' clock position whenever possible. As the aircraft overflies the target, a last fix is made by MAD equipment and by triggering the command-active buoy before the ASW weapons are released.

If homing torpedoes are used, these are dropped ahead of the submarine to give them time to dive to the required depth while homing.

Dropping from astern makes it more difficult to intercept a nuclear submarine making 40 knots plus underwater, and which can be very evasive when under attack, being 'flown' by a pilot using an aircraft-type control column, rudder pedals and a primary reference indicator similar to an attitude/horizon indicator.

The homing torpedo used by the Nimrod is the Marconi Sting Ray, and the depth charge is the British Aerospace Mk 11 Mod 3, which has a maximum depth of 295 ft and a 176 lb high-explosive warhead.

The aircraft is also cleared to carry the American B57 tactical gravity bomb, an air-dropped nuclear depth bomb whose warhead has a variable yield of between five and ten kilotons and which can operate at a depth of about 3,380 ft, sufficient to obliterate the deepest-diving submarine.

# CHAPTER FIFTEEN

# STORM FROM THE SEA

**A**s our soldiers were hesitating, mostly because of the depth of the water, the man who carried the Eagle of the Tenth Legion started praying to the gods that his act would bring good luck to the legion, shouted out loudly, "Jump down men, unless you want to betray your Eagle to the enemy. I at any rate shall have done my duty to my country and my general!"

'With these words he flung himself from the ship and began to carry the Eagle towards the enemy. Then the soldiers jumped down from the ship all together, urging each other not to allow a disgrace like that to happen...'

*The date was August, in the year 55 BC, the words were Julius Caesar's, describing the first Roman expedition to the island of Britain. There had been occasions before when ships had been used to transport armies to the shores of a hostile country, but this was probably the first instance when heavily-armed troops had been compelled to storm ashore in the face of fierce opposition. It would by no means be the last.*

*Since Caesar's day, amphibious warfare operations have been a feature of almost every conflict where sea has separated the belligerents.*

*By the time of the Napoleonic Wars, Britain's Royal Marines were a well-established and highly disciplined force, with contingents deployed on*

Allied landing craft on exercise, just prior to the D-Day landings in 1944. When the assault came it was a complete surprise to the Germans.

US Marines wade ashore in the Philippines, 1944. Such island assaults were very costly and many died.

ships of the line to form the nucleus of landing forces; the French had no such marine infantry, and consequently all their amphibious operations had to be under-taken by units of proper seamen or by army detachments who were not trained for service at sea - often with disastrous results.

Oddly enough, it was not until the First World War that ships were specially adapted to take assault infantry ashore. The first such vessel to be used in action was the SS River Clyde which, on 25 April 1915, disembarked troops at Gallipoli via special gangways, under the covering fire of machine-guns mounted behind sandbags in her bow.

Despite this, the disembarking infantry suffered terrible casualties. The same was true when British troops stormed the German U-Boat base at Zeebrugge, Belgium, on St George's Day 1918; here, the main assault vessel was the cruiser HMS Vindictive, which was fitted with 18 gangways and equipped with flame throwers and howitzers for close-range work against German shore batteries.

In 1940, the concept of amphibious warfare underwent a revolution with the formation of the first British Commando units and the development of the vessels that were to carry them into action. Converted fast cargo ships became assault carrier ships, while assault landing craft were developed, some to carry troops, others to lift tanks and heavy support vehicles.

The concept was put to the test in a series of raids on the German-held Lofoten Islands in March 1941, where little opposition was encountered; it was a different story at Dieppe in August 1942, when British and Canadian forces were decimated by powerful enemy resistance. Nevertheless, that disastrous raid laid the basis of further amphibious warfare developments, which were put to good use in the biggest assault operation of all time, the D-Day landings in Normandy, June 1944.

But it was in the vast ocean reaches of the Pacific that amphibious warfare came into its own, and established an undying reputation for the United States Marine Corps. This formation, despite a distinguished 170-year history, had no experience of major amphibious landings against strongly defended enemy territory, having previously served mainly as landing troops in naval operations, as boarding parties, or as guards for naval stations.

The cornerstone of their reputation was laid on 20 November 1943, when they stormed the heavily-defended Tarawa Atoll in the Gilbert Islands and took it in 76 hours of stark and bitter fighting. It was Tarawa, more than any other battle, more, even, than Okinawa and Iwo Jima, which was to give the US Marines a tradition of courage in battle that still held good nearly five decades later, when they stormed into occupied Kuwait as part of the Allied coalition forces.

# AWAY ALL BOATS Amphibious warfare in action

THE 1982 Falklands War proved that the amphibious task force is still one of the most effective methods of projecting power over long distances, just as it was in the Second World War. Indeed, in the case of the Falklands it was the only means of force projection at Britain's disposal.

That conflict also highlighted one major disadvantage of the amphibious assault. It is relatively slow in its approach to its objective, and vulnerable in the disembarkation phase. The British forces used six *Sir Lancelot* and *Sir Bedivere*-class Logistic Landing Ships (LSL) during the Falklands War, and two of them - the *Sir Galahad* and *Sir Tristram* - were severely damaged by Argentinian bombs during the landings at Bluff Cove, the former so severely that it later had to be sunk.

## FROM LSDLS TO LCCS'S

Apart from LSLs, which have doors and ramps built into their bow and stern to give a roll on/roll off capability, the principal types of amphibious warfare ships in use today are the LSD (Landing Ship Dock),

LPD (Amphibious Transport Dock), LHA (General Purpose Amphibious Assault Ship), LPH (Amphibious Assault Ship Helicopter), LHD (Multi-Purpose Amphibious Assault Ship) and LCC (Amphibious Command Ship).

LSDs include the US Navy's *Whidbey Island* and *Anchorage*-class vessels. The former can carry 21 Marine Landing Craft, 64 amphibious assault vehicles or four hovercraft, and has a raised flight deck that can be used by helicopters as large as the Sikorsky CR-53E Sea Stallion. It also has refuelling facilities for AV-8B Harriers. Eight ships of this type are in US Navy service, with four more on order. The *Anchorage*-class LSDs are from the earlier *Thomaston*-class, which were designed during the Korean War and which are now being replaced by the *Whidbey Island*-class ships. *Anchorage* can carry

*The assault ship USS* Tarawa *seen off the Philippines during the 1980 'Valiant Blitz' exercise. Note the large barn doors in the stern of the vessel.*

21 Marine Landing Craft or 50 amphibious assault vehicles. LSDs were originally developed during the Second World War for carrying heavy vehicles and landing craft.

The LPD is a further development of the LSD, with increased troop and vehicle capacity. LPDs in service with the US Navy are the *Raleigh* and *Austin* classes. One of the former, the USS *La Salle*, was converted to become the flagship of the Command Middle East Force (COMIDEASTFOR), serving with the US task forces in the Indian Ocean, and as such played a prominent part in the Gulf War.

Of all the amphibious assault ships deployed in the Gulf, the most impressive were undoubtedly the *Tarawa*-class General Purpose Amphibious Assault Ships, the largest of their type ever built. They displace 39,000 tons fully laden and, as well as carrying 160 tracked vehicles, artillery pieces and trucks, together with 40 amphibious personnel carriers, their hangar deck can accommodate 30 CH-46 Sea Night or 19 CH-53 Sea Stallion helicopters. The ships can also operate the Harrier and the OV-10A Bronco forward air control aircraft. Troop capacity is 1,000 Marines - a full battalion - and there is a fully equipped hospital with 300 beds. The three *Tarawa*-class vessels in USN service are fitted with the Tactical Amphibious Warfare Data System (TAWDS), as well as a satellite communications system and datalinks, enabling them to exercise command and control over the assault group's aircraft, weapons, sensors and landing craft.

**HELICOPTER-DEDICATED SHIPS**

The US Navy's main helicopter assault ships (LPD) are the *Iwo Jima*-class, of which seven units are in service. With a 600 ft flight deck, they can operate up to seven CH-46 or four CH-53 helicopters simultaneously, and their hangar deck can accommodate 19 CH-46s or 11 CH-53s. As they are dedicated to helicopter-borne assault, ships of this class do not carry landing craft.

The LPD Multi-Purpose Assault Ships of the US Navy, the 40,000 ton *Wasp* class, are based on the earlier *Tarawa* class. They can carry over 2,000 Marines in an emergency, and have normal accommodation for 1,000. The two *Wasp*-class vessels - the other is the USS *Essex* - have an air group comprising six AV-8B Harriers and about 30 helicopters, including Sea Knights, Super Stallions

*The US Navy's* Newport-*class LSTs, one of which is seen here on exercise in the Pacific, represents the ultimate in tank landing ship design.*

and Cobras. The maximum helicopter load is 42 Sea Knights.

The US Navy has two Amphibious Command Ships (LCC), the *Blue Ridge* and the *Mount Whitney*. These vessels are equipped to integrate air, land and sea assault operations and are fitted with an Amphibious Command Information System (ACIS), a Naval Intelligence Processing System (NIPS) and the Naval Tactical Data System (NTDS), all of which provide a comprehensive computerized tactical display.

The 19,200 ton ships also carry a satellite communications system, as well as extensive on-board photographic and document processing labs. Finally, the US amphibious forces have 20 of the world's most advanced LSTs or Tank Landing Ships. These 8,450 ton *Newport*-class vessels can carry 430 troops and a wide variety of assault craft. Their pointed bow enables them to sustain a speed of 20 knots, a requirement set for all US amphibious warfare ships, and is fitted with a 112 ft long aluminium ramp which can carry a 75 ton load.

Several of these vessels stood ready in the Gulf, ready to disgorge their M 60 tanks into Kuwait. The Iraqis fully expected it would happen. But the assault came from the land; the Allied surprise was complete.

# LYNX AND SEA SKUA The missile boat destroyer

**O**N 30 January 1991, a Westland Lynx helicopter on combat air patrol over the northern waters of the Gulf detected a real threat to the Allied task force: a TNC-45 fast patrol boat.

The vessel, then in Iraqi hands, had formerly belonged to the Kuwaiti Navy and was armed with Exocet sea-skimming anti-ship missiles. The Lynx, from HMS *Gloucester*, closed in for the attack and launched one of its Sea Skua missiles. Seconds later, the enemy boat was a smouldering wreck in the water.

The main purpose behind the development and deployment of anti-ship missiles is to eliminate enemy naval weapons systems before they become threats. It was for this purpose that British Aerospace developed the Sea Skua, the only missile in the western world designed to take the offensive against small, fast and highly manoeuvrable attack craft.

## ANATOMY OF A SEA SKUA ATTACK

To keep an enemy fast attack craft out of range of a capital ship, the Sea Skua has to be deployed well out beyond the ship itself; for this purpose it is mounted on the Royal Navy's Lynx, which carries four missiles per helicopter. When a target is located, the helicopter pilot sets a radar altimeter to allow the missile to skim just above the water, then launches it while still well outside the enemy's defences. The Sea Skua, which can be pre-set to fly at different heights, is only nine and a half feet long. It cruises at high subsonic speed under the power of its solid fuel rocket motor, and has a range of about ten miles. The missile has a semi-active radar homing seeker and operates in conjunction with the Lynx's Sea Spray radar, which illuminates the target.

The Lynx and Sea Skua combination first came into its own during the 1982 Falklands War, when the sea-skimming missiles disabled the Argentine supply vessel *Rio Carcarana* and later disabled a patrol craft, blasting away its entire bridge structure and killing eight crew. It was therefore with some confidence that the Royal Navy's Lynx crews undertook their vital task of providing a defensive screen for the Allied task force in the Gulf nine years later.

The first anti-surface vessel operation in the Gulf took place on 24 January 1991, when a Lynx from

*Arming a Royal Navy Lynx helicopter on HMS* London *prior to a CAP in the northern Gulf during* Operation Desert Storm.

## HUNTING WITH THE LYNX

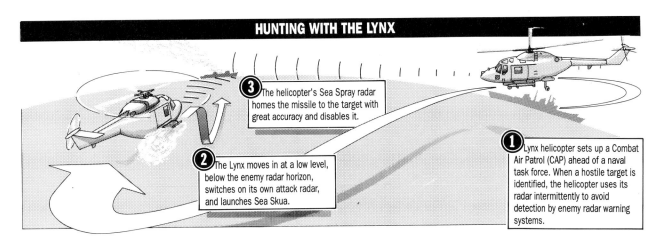

**3** The helicopter's Sea Spray radar homes the missile to the target with great accuracy and disables it.

**2** The Lynx moves in at a low level, below the enemy radar horizon, switches on its own attack radar, and launches Sea Skua.

**1** Lynx helicopter sets up a Combat Air Patrol (CAP) ahead of a naval task force. When a hostile target is identified, the helicopter uses its radar intermittently to avoid detection by enemy radar warning systems.

HMS *Cardiff* detected three Iraqi vessels - an Inshore minesweeper, patrol boat and landing craft - and called in US Navy A-6E Intruders to deal with them. The Intruders sank the patrol boat and landing craft, and the Iraqis scuttled the minesweeper to avoid capture.

Then, on the evening of 29 January, a US Navy SH-60B helicopter detected a flotilla of 17 small craft heading south off Maradin Island, close to the Saudi-Kuwait border. They were engaged by Lynx from HMS *Brazen* and HMS *Gloucester*, which sank four of the enemy craft with their Sea Skuas. 12 more were damaged in further attacks by AH-l Cobras and A-6Es. HMS *Cardiff*'s Lynx also found and sank a large patrol boat further south.

All these craft were believed to be ferrying troops to join an Iraqi land attack mounted later on the Saudi coastal town of Ras Al Khafji.

The next day saw the destruction of the Exocet-armed TNC-45 patrol boat, but that was not the Lynx's only triumph on 30 January. *Gloucester*'s helicopter also attacked a T43 minelayer, the Sea Skua exploding on target to leave the vessel burning and dead in the water.

In the estuary leading to Umm Qasr, HMS *Cardiff*'s Lynx severely damaged another T43 in a Sea Skua attack. US Navy pilots had something of a field day too, when A-6Es and F-18 Hornets fell on a group of eight Iraqi fast patrol craft - including *Osa*-class missile boats - outside Kuwait harbour and sank four, damaging a further three.

### MORE LYNX SUCCESSES

There was another Lynx success on the last day of January, resulting from a Sea Skua attack on an *Osa*-class boat near Bubiyan Island. The boat returned fire before exploding and sinking.

The Lynx were in action again on 1 February,

when helicopters from HMS *Gloucester* and HMS *London* attacked and disabled another Exocet-armed TNC-45, and on 11 February, when HMS *Cardiff*'s Lynx sank a Russian-built *Zhuk*-class fast patrol boat. This was a night-time engagement in which the Lynx's Sandpiper forward-looking infra-red sighting system was used operationally for the first time. Another fast patrol craft was sunk by a Lynx from the Type 42 destroyer HMS *Manchester* later in the day, and on 16 February, in the last such action of the Gulf War, a Sea Skua disabled what must surely have been the Iraqi Navy's only surviving patrol craft.

Throughout the Gulf War, the Royal Navy Lynx crews operated in a difficult and hostile environment far in advance of the Allied naval forces. They faced a demanding task, and they performed it extraordinarily well.

*An artist's impression of a ship-launched Sea-Skua that is undergoing testing. In the Gulf War, Sea Skua proved itself a very able weapon.*

# GLOSSARY

**AA** Anti-Aircraft

**AAA** Anti-Aircraft Artillery

**AAM** Air-to-Air Missile

**ABM** Anti-Ballistic Missile missile

**ACR** Advanced Combat Rifle

**ADP** Automatic Data Processing - a system whereby information is processed by computer and presented for analysis in display form.

**ADF** Air Defence Variant (of the Panavia Tornado)

**AEW** Airborne Early Warning

**AFV** Armoured Fighting Vehicle

**ALARM** Air-Launched Anti-Radiation Missile - a British Aerospace weapon that homes in on enemy radar transmissions to destroy the sites.

**AMRAAM** Advanced Medium-Range Air-to-Air Missile

**ARBS** Angle Rate Bombing System - a weapons release system fitted to the AV-8B Harrier II.

**ASM** Air-to-Surface Missile

**ASRAAM** Advanced Short-Range Air-to-Air Missile

**ASV** Air to Surface Vessel - airborne detection radar for locating ships and submarines.

**ASW** Anti-Submarine Warfare

**ATF** Advanced Tactical Fighter. The US Aerospace Industry has produced two ATF designs to meet a requirement for an F-15 Eagle replacement. These are the Lockheed YF-22 and the Northrop YF-23. Both are highly agile and incorporate a great deal of 'stealth' technology. In April 1991, after intensive trials, the USAF announced that the YF-22 had been selected. Production of 750 aircraft is to start in 1996.

**ATGW** Anti-Tank Guided Weapon.

**AVRE** Armoured Vehicle Royal Engineers - a tank chassis mounting combat engineering equipment such as bulldozer blade, mine plough etc.

**AWACS** Airborne Warning and Control System - the Boeing E-3 Sentry, for example, or the Grumman E-2 Hawkeye.

**BMF** Battlefield Management System - a computerized system fitted in the M1 Abrams that processes and analyses information received by the tank's sensory systems for the benefit of the commander.

**CAP** Combat Air Patrol.

**CEP** Circular Error Probable - a measure of the accuracy attributable to ballistic missiles, bombs and shells. It is the radius of a circle into which 50 per cent of the missiles aimed at the centre of the circle are expected to fall.

**Clutter** A term used in radar parlance to describe reflected echoes on a cathode ray tube caused by the ground, sea, bad weather etc.

**CPB** Charged Particle Beam - a stream of charged atomic particles of intense energy, focused on a target.

**ECM** Electronic Countermeasures - systems designed to confuse and disrupt enemy radar equipment.

**ECCM** Electronic Counter-Countermeasures - measures taken to reduce the effectiveness of ECM by improving the resistance of radar equipment to jamming.

**ECR** Electronic Combat Reconnaissance - a variant of the Panavia Tornado optimized for electronic warfare.

**ELF** Extremely Low Frequency - a radio frequency used for communications with submarines.

**ELINT** Electronic Intelligence - information gathered through monitoring enemy electronic transmissions by specially-equipped aircraft, ships or satellites.

**ELW** Electronic Warfare

**FAC** Forward Air Controller - a battlefront observer who directs strike aircraft on to targets near the front line.

**FAE** Fuel-Air Explosive - a weapon that disperses fuel into the atmosphere in the form of an aerosol cloud above a target. The cloud is ignited to produce intense blast and heat effects.

**FEBA** Forward Edge of the Battle Area

**FGA** Fighter Ground Attack aircraft

**FLIR** Forward-Looking Infra-Red - heat-sensing equipment fitted in an aircraft that scans the path ahead to detect heat from objects such as vehicle engines etc.

**FOFA** Follow-on Forces Attack - strategy whereby reinforcements heading for the battle area are subjected to heavy attack by aircraft, missiles etc.

**FROG** Free-flight Rocket Over Ground - a rocket that follows a ballistic trajectory without the aid of specialized guidance equipment.

**FRS** Fighter Reconnaissance Strike (as in Sea Harrier FRS2)

**GR** General Reconnaissance (as in Tornado GR1)

**Geo-synchronous** the orbit of a satellite whose position over a given location on the earth remains the same by synchronizing the satellite's orbital speed with the earth's rotation. Also called geostationary.

**GPS** Global Positioning System - a system of American navigational satellites.

**HE** High Explosive

**HEAT** High Explosive Anti-Tank

**HESH** High Explosive Squash Head

**HF** High Frequency (radio waves)

**HOTAS** Hands-on-Throttle-and-Stick - a system whereby the pilot exercises full control over his aircraft in combat without the need to remove his hands from throttle and control column in order to change weapons selection switches etc.

**HUD** Head-Up Display - system in which essential information is projected on to a cockpit windscreen so that the pilot has no need to look down at his instrument panel.

**ICBM** Intercontinental Ballistic Missile

**IFF** Identification Friend or Foe - an electronic pulse emitted by an aircraft to identify it as friendly on a radar screen.

**INF** Intermediate Range Nuclear Forces

**INS** Inertial Navigation System - an on-board guidance system that steers an aircraft or missile over a pre-determined course by measuring factors such as the distance travelled, reference to 'waypoints' (landmarks), en route etc.

**Interdiction** Deep air strikes into enemy rear areas to sever communications with the battlefield.

**IR**: Infra-Red.

**Jamming** Tactics involving the disruption of enemy radio and radar transmissions by electronic or other means.

**JSTARS** Joint Surveillance and Target Attack Radar System - an airborne command and control system that directs air and ground forces in battle.

**JTACMS** Joint Tactical Missile System - a long-range artillery missile designed to be fired by existing Multiple Launch Rocket Systems.

**Kiloton** Nuclear weapon yield, one kiloton (KT) being roughly equivalent to 1,000 tons of TNT conventional explosive.

**LAMPS** Light Airborne Multi-Purpose System - anti-submarine helicopter equipment comprising search radar, sonobuoys and other detection equipment.

**LANTIRN** Low-Altitude Navigation and Targeting Infra-Red for Night - an infra-red system fitted to the F-15E Strike Eagle that combines heat sensing with terrain-following radar to enable the pilot to view the ground ahead of the aircraft during low-level night operations. The information is projected on to his head-up display.

**LAW** Light Anti-Tank Weapon (such as a man-portable missile launcher).

**LF** Low Frequency (radio waves)

**LWR** Laser Warning Radar - equipment fitted to an aircraft that warns the pilot if he is being tracked by a missile-guiding laser beam.

**Mach Number** The ratio of the speed of an aircraft or missile to the local speed of sound. At sea level, Mach One (1.0M) is approximately 762 mph, decreasing to about 660 mph at 30,000 ft. An aircraft or missile travelling faster than Mach One is said to be supersonic. Mach numbers are dependent on variations in atmospheric temperature and pressure and are registered on a Machmeter in an aircraft's cockpit. The formula takes its name from the scientist who first devised it, Dr Ernst Mach.

**MAD** Magnetic Anomaly Detection. The passage of a large body of metal, such as a submarine, through the Earth's magnetic field, causes disturbances which can be detected by special equipment in an anti-submarine warfare aircraft.

**MBT** Main Battle Tank - classification of heavy armoured fighting vehicles including the M1 Abrams, Challenger and Challenger 2.

**Megaton** Thermonuclear weapon yield, one megaton (MT3 being roughly equal to 1,000,000 tons of TNT).

**MG** Machine Gun

**MIRV** Multiple Independently-Targeted Re-entry Vehicle - a system in which several warheads are carried into space by a single ballistic missile, then separated on re-entering the Earth's atmosphere to attack different targets.

**MLRS** Multiple Launch Rocket System - a mobile artillery system that launches rockets carrying fragmentation warheads.

**MV** Muzzle Velocity - the speed at which a bullet or shell leaves the gun barrel.

**NEC** Nuclear, Chemical and Biological Warfare

**NORAD** North American Air Defence Command - a combined US and Canadian command responsible for world-wide surveillance and early warning of conventional or nuclear attack on the North American continent.

**NVG** Night Vision Goggles - specially designed goggles that enhance a pilot's ability to see at night.

**OBOGS** On-Board Oxygen Generating System - a system installed in the AV-8B Harrier II that generates oxygen, avoiding the need to rely on pre-charged oxygen bottles and extending the time a pilot can remain airborne during, say, long transit flights over the ocean.

**Phased-Array Radar** A warning radar system using many small aerials spread over a large flat area, rather than a rotating scanner. The advantage of this system is that it can track hundreds of targets simultaneously, electronically redirecting its beam from target to target in a matter of microseconds (millionths of a second).

**PLSS** Precision Location Strike System - a battlefield surveillance system installed in the Lockheed TR-1 that detects the movement of enemy forces and directs air and ground attacks against them.

**POL** Petrol, Oil and Lubricants.

**Pulse-Doppler Radar** a type of airborne interception radar that picks out fast-moving targets from background clutter by measuring the change in frequency of a series of pulses bounced off the targets. This is based on the well-known Doppler effect, an apparent change in the frequency of waves when the source emitting them has a relative velocity towards or away from an observer. The most famous example of this effect is a train whistle, which seems to rise, reach a crescendo as the train passes the observer, and then recede. The MiG-29's famous tail-slide manoeuvre is a tactical move designed to break the lock of a pulse-Doppler radar.

**RWR** Radar Warning Receiver - a device mounted on an aircraft that warns the pilot if he is being tracked by an enemy missile guidance or air intercept radar.

**SAM** Surface-to-Air Missile

**SAS** Special Air Service - British special forces' troops.

**SDI** Strategic Defense Initiative - also known as 'Star Wars', is designed to provide an effective shield against nuclear missile attack by the use of very high technology defences.

**SEAL** Sea, Air and Land commands - US special forces' troops.

**SHF** Super High Frequency (radio waves)

**SIGINT** Signals Intelligence - the assembling of information on enemy intentions by monitoring electronic transmissions from his command, control and communications network.

**SLAM** Stand-Off Land Attack Missile - a missile that can be air-launched many miles from the target area.

**SLAR** Side-Looking Airborne Radar - a type of radar that provides a continuous radar map of the ground on either side of the aircraft carrying the equipment.

**SOSUS** Sound Surveillance System - a network of American sound detection equipment positioned on the sea bed to track submarines.

**SSBN** Sub-Surface Ballistic Nuclear-classification denoting a nuclear-powered strategic missile submarine)

**SSN** Sub-Surface Nuclear-classification denoting nuclear-powered submarine armed with torpedoes for anti-ship and hunter-killer operations).

**Stealth Technology** Modern technology applied to aircraft or fighting vehicles to reduce their radar signatures by cutting down the number of reflective surfaces etc. Examples of stealth aircraft are the Lockheed F-117 A and the Northrop B-2 bomber.

**TADS** Target Acquisition/Designation System - a laser sighting system fitted to the AH-64 attack helicopter.

**TPGSM** Terminally-Guided Sub-Munitions-small anti-armour missiles which, deployed from a warhead, locate and home on to their targets.

**Thermal Imagers** Equipment fitted to an aircraft or tank which typically comprises a telescope to collect and focus infra-red energy emitted by objects on a battlefield, a mechanism to scan the scene across an array of heat-sensitive detectors, and a processor to turn the signals from these detectors into a 'thermal image' displayed on a TV screen.

**TIALD** Thermal Imaging/Airborne Laser Designator - equipment fitted to the Tornado GR1 enabling it to locate and attack precision targets at night.

**TOW** Tube-Launched, Optically-tracked, Wire-guided anti-tank missile.

**VHF** Very High Frequency (radio waves)

**VLF** Very Low Frequency (radio waves)

**Warsaw Pact** The now-defunct military alliance between the Soviet Union and its Eastern European allies, formed as a counter to the NATO alliance.

**Window** Strips of tinfoil cut to the wavelengths of enemy warning and missile radars and scattered from attacking aircraft to confuse enemy defences. Also known as 'chaff'.

# INDEX

Page numbers in italic refer to illustrations.

# ACKNOWLEDGEMENTS

Eddison Sadd acknowledge their special thanks to Nigel Bradley who edited, designed and produced this book on an Apple Macintosh DTP system, and to Phil Green who organized the team of artwork artists.

Robert Jackson would like to acknowledge the help he has had from many quarters in writing this book and singles out for special mention: Veronica Shutes of Thorn EMI Electronics; Andrew Jeacock of Royal Ordnance plc; Mike Edwards of Marconi Underwater Systems Ltd; Simon Raynes of British Aerospace Dynamics Ltd; Brian Trueman of Vickers Defence Systems Ltd; and Bob Archer and Dennis Doble of Pearson Engineering.

Nigel Bradley wishes to thank Teddy Neville of TRH Pictures; Major RCM Thorn and Corporal C Jackson; Sgt T Prine, 48th TFW PA Office; Frank Randell, Jnr, RAF Mildenhall PA Office and Richard Colley, RAF Upper Heyford PA Office.

Artwork: Gary Cook, Ian Moores and Chris Sargent.
Proof Readers: Hilary Dickinson and Cecilia Walters.
Indexer: Michael Allaby.
Production: Hazel Kirkman & Charles James.

**Photographic credits:** Title page TRH/DoD; opposite verso TRH/US Navy; opposite Contents MoD; 8 Nigel Bradley; 10-11 TRH/Alan Landau; 12 Robert Jackson; 13 Robert Jackson; 14-15 all British Aerospace exept 15 lower left Nigel Bradley; 16 TRH/USAF; 17 Zeefa; 17-18 British Aerospace; 20 Robert Jackson; 21 Nigel Bradley; 23 Nigel Bradley; 24 Zefa; 25 British Aerospace; 26 USAF; 27 Nigel Bradley; 30 Robert Jackson; 31 top Robert Jackson, British Aerospace; 32 McDonnell Douglas via Nigel Bradley; 33 TRH/Martin Marietta; 34 TRH/ Grumman; 35 Nigel Bradley; 30 both Robert Jackson; 31 Zefa; 42; TRH/SMP 87; 44 Nigel Bradley; 45 TRH/DoD; 46 TRH/MBB; 47 both TRH/DoD; 46 TRH/Euromissile; 49 TRH/Canadair; 50 Robert Jackson; 51 Robert Jackson; 52 Nigel Bradley; 53 British Aerospace, top Nigel Bradley; 54 TRH/Rockwell; 55 Nigel Bradley; 56-57 MoD; 58-59 Robert Jackson, 60 TRH/British Aerospace; 61 TRH/USAF; 62 Nigel Bradley; 63 Patrick Allen; 64 Nigel Bradley; 68 TRH/US Army; 69 TRH; 70 TRH/DoD; 71 TRH/ Mike Roberts; 73 via Robert Jackson; 74 British Aerospace; 75 top, TRH/Euromissile, British Aerospace; 76 TRH/IWM; 77 both TRH; 78 TRH/E Neville; TRH/DoD; 80-83 all Pearson Engineering; 84 top, TRH, TRH/IWM; 88 via Robert Jackson;

90 TRH/DoD; 92-93 all Robert Jackson; 94-95 TRH/US Navy; 97 both TRH/DoD; 99 TRH/DoD; 100-101 TRH/US Navy; 102 Robert Jackson; 103 TRH/Royal Navy; 105 TRH/US Navy; 106-107 TRH/Grumman; 108-109 both TRH/DoD; 112 TRH; 112 TRH/Royal Navy HMS Neptune; 115 TRH/US Navy; 116 British Aerospace; 118 TRH/US Navy, centre TRH/Royal Navy; 119 TRH/US Navy; 122 Robert Jackson; 123 TRH/Royal Navy; 125 TRH/SMP 84; 126 top TRH/SMP 84, TRH/Vickers; 129 Marconi Underwater Systems Ltd; 130-131 TRH/US Navy; 132 -133 Robert Jackson; 134 TRH/SMP 87; 135 TRH/DoD; 136-137 TRH/Lockheed; 138 TRH/E Neville; 139 TRH/Sikorsky; 140-141 TRH/E Neville; 142 TRH; 143 Robert Jackson; 144 TRH/DoD; 145 TRH/US Navy; 148 Patrick Allen; 147 British Aerospace.